NEW DIRECTIONS
FOR
PHILANTHROPIC
FUNDRAISING

Dwight F. Burlingame, Timothy L. Seiler,
Eugene R. Tempel
*Indiana University Center on Philanthropy*
EDITORS

# DEVELOPING
# MAJOR GIFTS

Dwight F. Burlingame
*Indiana University Center on Philanthropy*
James M. Hodge
*Mayo Foundation for Medical Education and Research*

EDITORS

**NUMBER 16, SUMMER 1997**

DEVELOPING MAJOR GIFTS
*Dwight F. Burlingame, James M. Hodge* (eds.)
New Directions for Philanthropic Fundraising, No. 16, Summer 1997
*Dwight F. Burlingame, Timothy L. Seiler, Eugene R. Tempel,* Editors

NEW DIRECTIONS FOR PHILANTHROPIC FUNDRAISING is indexed in Higher Education
Abstracts and Philanthropic Index.

Microfilm copies of issues and articles are available in 16 mm and 35 mm, as well as
microfiche in 105 mm, through University Microfilms Inc., 300 North Zeeb Road,
Ann Arbor, Michigan 48106-1346.

ISSN 1072-172X    ISBN 0-7879-9855-9

NEW DIRECTIONS FOR PHILANTHROPIC FUNDRAISING is part of The Jossey-Bass
Nonprofit Sector Series and is published quarterly by Jossey-Bass Inc., Publishers,
350 Sansome Street, San Francisco, California 94104-1342.

SUBSCRIPTIONS cost $67.00 for individuals and $115.00 for institutions, agencies,
and libraries. Prices subject to change. Refer to the Ordering Information page
at the back of this issue.

EDITORIAL CORRESPONDENCE should be sent to the editor, Dwight F. Burlingame,
Center on Philanthropy, Indiana University, 550 West North Street, Suite 301,
Indianapolis, IN 46202–3162.

Jossey-Bass Web address: http://www.josseybass.com

Printed in the United States of America on acid-free recycled paper containing 100
percent recovered waste paper, of which at least 20 percent is postconsumer waste.

# Contents

# Editors' Notes

MANAGERS OF VOLUNTARY and philanthropic sector organizations often remark that fundraising is getting increasingly more difficult. Factors contributing to this environment are the burgeoning number of charitable organizations competing for philanthropic dollars, cutbacks in government support, and the decrease in available volunteer hours. The importance of major gifts to the life of nonprofits has therefore taken on greater urgency.

Understanding the context and the role of major gifts is the focus of this issue. Our authors have taken a new look at many of the questions facing organizations today, from what makes a good major gifts professional to the motivations of major donors. The authors provide an updated guide to many of these important issues in the field of philanthropic fundraising as we enter a new century.

Although planned gifts are generally considered a component of major gifts, we have by design not included a detailed discussion of planned gifts in this issue. Likewise, we have chosen not to discuss development research or prospect information; these topics will be covered in future issues.

Woven throughout "Major Gifts" is a unifying theme that brings us back to the value of relationship building and the importance of integrity and ethics in major gift fundraising. In Chapter One, Ernest W. Wood begins the issue by identifying characteristics and skills that exemplify effective major gift fundraisers. His thesis is important for philanthropic boards and managers to consider as they seek to attract and retain outstanding fundraisers.

Jerry A. May reviews the internal management of the major gift fundraising process, with an eye to increasing overall fundraising results. Chapter Two encourages us to keep donor interests front

NEW DIRECTIONS FOR PHILANTHROPIC FUNDRAISING, NO. 16, SUMMER 1997 © JOSSEY-BASS PUBLISHERS

and center as the most important value in major gift fundraising as well as holding the major gift process as the focus of all fundraising efforts.

In Chapter Three, Paul B. Smith takes the management of the major gifts process to a new level by relaying in detail the cultivation cycle necessary to bring about successful major gift fundraising. Much of this chapter details the relevance of management theory to today's major gifts program.

In the fourth chapter, Joseph S. Beyel reflects on important ethical issues that face major gift fundraisers today. He deals not only with the seeking of gifts but with questions of whether and when it is appropriate to accept specific types of major gifts offered to institutions.

Martha A. Taylor and Sondra C. Shaw, the authors of Chapter Five, remind us that American women own 60 percent of the wealth in the United States. Fundraising directed toward women will not be successful if it employs a male-dominated model of major gifts. Involving women early and intensively as major benefactors in the mission and continuously cultivating relationships with these benefactors are two essentials in achieving success in raising major gifts from women.

G. T. "Buck" Smith demonstrates that major gift fundraising is a responsibility not only of the major gift officer but also of directors, board members, presidents, deans, and indeed all advocates for a nonprofit organization. How to enlist the best efforts from these various constituencies is the focus of Chapter Six.

In the final chapter, Paul G. Schervish provides an insightful look at what motivates major donors. How can professionals work with individuals of significant wealth who want to feel they are making a big difference in the nonprofit arena?

Quite simply, some organizations will not survive the new and competitive nonprofit environment of the twenty-first century. Gaining strategic advantage may require all of us in the profession to look back on some of the tried-and-true methods of developing major gifts as well as to acknowledge that "business as usual" in the major gift arena will not be good enough in the years ahead.

Capturing your prospective donors' attention, developing essential donor relationships, and managing the major gift focus in your office determine if your organization will flourish or fade in the years ahead.

Dwight F. Burlingame
James M. Hodge
*Editors*

DWIGHT F. BURLINGAME *is director of academic programs and research at the Indiana University Center on Philanthropy, Indianapolis, and professor of philanthropic studies.*

JAMES M. HODGE *is development officer at the Mayo Foundation for Medical Education and Research in Rochester, Minnesota.*

*This chapter explores the essential characteristics and skills that "qualify" major gift fundraisers, and the application of these traits to the process of acquiring major gifts.*

# 1

# Profiling major gifts fundraisers: What qualifies them for success

*Ernest W. Wood*

FOR AS LONG AS I CAN REMEMBER, a quote by architect Daniel Burnham has hung on my office wall. It reads: "Make no little plans. They have no magic to stir men's blood and probably themselves will not be realized. Make big plans; aim high in hope and work, remembering that a noble, logical diagram once recorded will never die, but long after we are gone will be a living thing, asserting itself with ever-growing insistency. Remember that our sons and grandsons are going to do things that would stagger us. Let your watchword be order and your beacon beauty. Think big."

Although I have been a philanthropic fundraiser for more than thirty-five years and consider some of the most successful major gift fundraisers around the world to be good friends and colleagues, there are thousands of others I have never met. I can assure you, though, that each one of them who has come to realize, as I have, that major gift fundraising is what they love doing most would quickly identify with Burnham's philosophy. Certainly there are skills, qualities, characteristics, and traits that contribute substantially to the makeup of an excellent major gift fundraiser. But it is

NEW DIRECTIONS FOR PHILANTHROPIC FUNDRAISING, NO. 16, SUMMER 1997 © JOSSEY-BASS PUBLISHERS

mind-set that is fundamental to being a successful long-term major gift fundraiser: thinking big; aiming high; and having a vision, an unwavering commitment to noble aspirations, and a passion for making the future better.

We do not have quantitative research data that substantiate a specific standard profile for a successful major gift fundraising professional, although some characteristics have been identified in interviews with recognized leaders in the field during related research projects. These insights, together with the knowledge many of us have gained over the years in the profession through experience and observation, have helped establish what I believe to be universally recognizable qualifications for a successful major gift fundraiser.

A list of the qualifications possessed by really good major gift fundraisers includes mind-set, character, education, background experience, skills, attitude, and personal values. How do people prepare for the profession? What educational requirements are needed? How should major gift fundraisers be evaluated? How do they do their work? What process do they follow in getting major gifts? What responsibilities do they have to the prospect and the donor? What do donors, their own institutions, and their professional colleagues expect of them?

The purpose of this article is to identify the essential characteristics and skills that "qualify" major gift fundraisers and describe the application of these traits to the process of acquiring major gifts.

Giving is a habit of the heart, not a tax deduction. Making a major gift is a personal and private decision that is always directly linked to the donor's values and needs. Engaging in the sensitive practice of major gift fundraising demands the highest level of trust, integrity, and ethics because it involves an intimate and unique exchange of values. Successful practitioners come to know that making a major gift can be one of the greatest and most meaningful experiences in a donor's life. Major gift philanthropy offers donors the opportunity to perpetuate their values beyond their own lifetime and allows their influence, memory, and life purpose to endure.

## *Integrity tops the list*

Without question, the overriding characteristic required for long-term success as a major gift fundraiser is integrity. Without it, one is doomed to failure. Integrity builds trust. The work of acquiring major gifts cannot be done outside an environment of trust. This has been substantiated as the number-one prerequisite for successful fundraising in numerous professional surveys, interviews, and research projects on the subject.

## *Mind-set: Think big, be positive, commit to mission and donor needs*

In addition to thinking big—having vision and noble aspirations—the mind-set of a major gift fundraiser must embrace high expectations, optimism, adventure, creative solutions, strategic visualization, positive approaches, and a strong commitment to understanding the organization's mission and the donor's needs. The clear focus on donor's needs, concerns, and values is always first and foremost, while the needs and mission of the institution to be served are second. This principle may occasionally create conflict, which forces integrity, ethics, and professional standards into play on the part of the fundraiser. Such circumstances often test the true character of the professional fundraiser, demanding integrity and courage to do what is right in the face of conflicting demands.

## *Character: Integrity, ethics, professional standards, and courage*

No respected major gift fundraiser works on a percentage or commission basis. Not only would this be in violation of the accepted *Code of Ethical Principles and Standards of Professional Practice* adopted by the membership of the National Society of Fundraising Executives, but such a practice is obviously a gross conflict of interest for the fundraiser. Rarely is any one person solely responsible for raising a major gift. Some of the largest gifts received on my watch as the chief development officer of a university were the result of years of cultivation and good stewardship by a predecessor, volunteer, or other member of the university staff. So how could I take 100 percent of the credit for such a gift?

If a fundraiser knows, for example, that the major gift an elderly woman is considering will overextend her resources to meet future personal needs such as health care, the fundraiser should act in the donor's best interest. In this situation, I always ask myself, "Is this something I would recommend that my own mother do?" This may not be a very popular position with the institution that pays the fundraiser's salary, nor does it enhance the immediate "dollars raised success record" of the fundraiser. However, if the fundraiser does not have the integrity to make the right ethical decision in such cases, the long-term outcomes can be extremely damaging to the donor, the institution, and the fundraiser.

There are times when a donor may want to make a gift designated to a program or purpose outside the organization's mission or beyond its ability to fulfill. If the organization cannot use the gift to fulfill its mission or deliver on the donor's designated purpose, the fundraiser must decline the gift and take the high road by helping the donor redirect the gift to another organization whose mission *is* compatible with the donor's designation or that *has* the ability to fulfill the donor's designated purpose. This does not appear to be in question when the gift is $5,000, but with $5 million it seems to take on a whole new meaning.

In rare situations, donors intentionally or otherwise want to attach certain illegal or unethical requirements to their gifts. When these circumstances cannot be rectified, the fundraiser must have the integrity to gently turn down the gift with an appropriate and helpful explanation.

These simple illustrations are realities in the life of the professional major gift fundraiser. Decisions and ethical practices are most often guided by the fundraiser's own mind-set, character, values, attitude, background experience, and deep personal convictions about the work and the institutions and people served. The debate regarding how one develops these qualities and characteristics is ongoing. What are the shaping factors: family, religion, education, professional experience, training, naturally inherited gifts? Or all of the above?

## *Education, values, and experience: Head, heart, and hand*

What does one need to know, feel, and experience to be a good major gift fundraiser? To put it another way, what do you need to have in your *head*, in your *heart*, and as part of your *hands-on* experience to be good at this kind of work? This is a difficult question to answer but one that continues to demand investigation and evaluation. It is my opinion, and apparently that of others who have made some inquiry, that the answers remain subjective but are borne out by experience.

There is no question that, beyond formal education, the personal qualities and experience a major gift fundraiser brings to his or her work are powerful factors for success. These assets, some of which are critical, include qualities such as self-confidence, self-esteem, self-motivation, aptitude for personal growth, controlled ego, sense of humor, strong work ethic, caring nature, commitment to something bigger than oneself, sense of community, civic responsibility, adventurous spirit, gentle tenacity, flexibility, positive attitude, tolerance for ambiguity, analytical reflection, inquisitive mind, creative talents, and other similar traits.

Are successful major gift fundraisers just naturally gifted? Or can they be educated and trained to do their jobs? As with other professionals, the truth is likely to be a strong combination of both. Even so, some intelligent people don't seem to have the aptitude or temperament no matter how much education or training they get. But for those who do, a sound education, good mentoring, and useful training are essential to fully develop and flourish in this work.

It has always been of interest to me that the best major gift fundraisers I know have strong religious roots. Some of them, like myself, have ministerial backgrounds. Curiously, these practitioners who bump shoulders with the philanthropic rich do not come from wealth but from families and educational institutions that place great emphasis on spiritual and ethical values. Although they are engaged in raising millions of dollars for worthy causes, their developmental values seem to center on principles of spiritual truth and a concern for others rather than business, profit, and money.

## The educational paradox

What educational preparation does a major gift fundraiser need? Where would someone aspiring to this field go to prepare for such a career? One of the true paradoxes in the historical growth of our profession is that although it was developed, institutionalized, and practiced at its highest level within institutions of higher education, these same colleges and universities whose degree of excellence— or very survival—is dependent on gift income have never seriously undertaken the task of creating educational programs to prepare students for such careers.

The four basic administrative divisions of higher education, traditionally represented by vice presidents, are academic, finance, student life, and institutional advancement or fundraising. For decades, students have been able to select an academic major to prepare for careers in all these divisions of higher education except fundraising. This paradox prompted me to research and write my doctoral dissertation, "A Model Graduate Curriculum in Fundraising Administration for American Higher Education," at a time when there were no such academic programs or centers on philanthropy.

Perhaps this situation existed for such a long time because none of us really set out to become fundraisers in the first place. We evolved or were sucked into it as a result of an existing need. However, this is beginning to change as younger professionally minded people see the opportunity, need, and potential for a career in the not-for-profit world that is rewarding, adventuresome, challenging, and meaningful.

The skills and knowledge needed to do our work well do not fall into any one educational track. The amazing spectrum of study and academic majors of successful major gift fundraisers is even more confusing. However, verbal and writing skills; the ability to motivate others; management skills; persuasive communications; entrepreneurship; understanding people; good listening skills; strategic thinking; and ability to comprehend legal, business, and financial matters, among other things, should give us some clue as to the type of educational courses needed to prepare for this work. Most of my colleagues would agree that a good values-based liberal arts education is an excellent foundation for preparing major gift fundraisers for their work. Graduate courses in business, psychology, theology, communications, management, education, philosophy, social science, leadership, literature, history, law, and of course philanthropy would all be helpful.

## Attitude and skills: Tools of the trade

It is difficult, if not impossible, to separate attitude and skills when determining what is required for doing effective major gift fundraising. As critical as they are, skills alone are not enough unless the fundraiser is optimistic; positive in spite of setbacks; accepting of problems as opportunities; and resilient in the face of obstacles, objections, and failure. A positive, realistic attitude is essential. This kind of attitude helps the fundraiser believe that prospects are *really* willing to give money away; that the work of their organization is absolutely essential in our society; and that fundraising is a marvelous and privileged calling that really makes a difference in our world. Certainly a key factor in accomplishing many of life's endeavors, attitude is of paramount importance in major gift fundraising.

### Listening

The skills needed for successful major gift fundraising are many. On the job, they are constantly being developed and improved. Because a number of the skills needed to be effective in this work have already been mentioned, I highlight the ones that need special emphasis. *Listening* is at the top of my list as probably the most important skill in major gift fundraising. Discovering the donor's needs and values must come before we can ask them to make a gift that meets their needs and values; discovery thus maximizes the gift level to be achieved. We do not learn anything about the donor if we do all the talking. Failing to listen is the biggest mistake unskilled fundraisers make during donor meetings.

### Negotiation

The pivotal moment, perhaps, is the "ask": for a gift in a specific "stretch" amount, for a specific project or purpose, to be paid over a specific period of time, and from assets you the fundraiser know exist. Yet as important as the ask may be, the greatest part of the work in getting a major gift comes long before the ask. Discovering helpful information about the prospect through research and donor meetings is essential if an intelligent ask is to be made. Then there is cultivating, educating, and informing the prospect about the organization and its goals and objectives. Finally, when the ask is made, the fundraiser should expect a "no" answer. This is when the skill of *negotiation* comes into play. The first task following a response of no is to discover what the prospect is saying no to. Is it the amount? The purpose? The pledge period? The use of certain assets? The fundraiser must first acknowledge and identify the objections being raised by listening and then begin to address those concerns through discussion and negotiation.

### Communication

Articulate and persuasive *communication* is a skill every good major gift fundraiser needs. Although writing skills are essential, this is one-on-one, face-to-face fundraising and not grant proposal writing. Good major gift fundraising is never a high-powered, fast-talking sales approach or arm-twisting session. It is providing an opportunity for the donor to make a gift that meets the donor's need first to perpetuate his or her values by way of your organization and second to make something good happen. Good listening, negotiating, and communication skills are very important in getting any major gift. These skills (coupled with a positive attitude) work equally well for the introverted or extroverted, quiet or exuberant fundraiser.

## *The four R's of major gift fundraising*

There is a strategic process that major gift fundraisers follow in obtaining stretch gifts from donors. Training programs that I have observed use from three to seventeen steps to explain and teach this process. Although I use a six-step strategic process when conducting major gift training seminars, I use my "four R's" of major gift fundraising here for conceptual reasons. They are Research, Romance, Request, and Recognition.

There is a wonderful parallel between major gift fundraising and courtship and marriage. As a normal courtship begins, the two parties need to discover a little bit about each other. In fundraising, this is called prospect *research*.

The next step in courtship involves introductions, encounters, meetings, and dating over a period of time. As the budding *romance* develops, the two parties discover their shared values, need for each other, feelings of devotion, fondness, and love. In fundraising, this is donor involvement and cultivation.

Before an actual ask ("Will you marry me?") takes place, there must be an established relationship that justifies such a *request*. Similarly, linkage and a sound relationship must exist between a donor and an organization before an ask is made. Asking for a gift from a prospect with whom the organization has no relationship is as inappropriate as asking for someone's hand in marriage without really knowing the person.

If the answer is yes and a marriage takes place, it represents an exchange of values and *recognition* of the commitment that has been made. A relationship remains strong through gratitude, appreciation, stewardship, continued romance, and commitment. Similarly, following a commitment to a gift, the organization must sustain all of the elements and intensity of the initial romance and relationship with the donor. Just as in a good courtship and marriage, a healthy ongoing gift relationship depends on an intimate and unique exchange of values based on trust, integrity, good communications, and all of the other characteristics that have been described.

## Institutional evaluation and expectation

Major gift fundraising is a long-term process. Lasting eighteen months on average, it takes at least three face-to-face meetings with the prospect: a discovery meeting, an ask meeting, and a negotiate-and-close meeting. Obviously, this relationship-building process and long-term effort to obtain major gifts cannot be evaluated annually in the same way that other fundraising programs might be (such as the number of gifts and the amount of money raised in the past twelve months).

Institutional expectations regarding the performance of a major gifts fundraiser should be based on an established set of criteria that include many of the characteristics and skills discussed in this chapter. Is the fundraiser actively planning and coordinating the contacting, cultivating, asking, negotiating, closing, and thanking of donors with volunteers, the president, and other staff? What progress is being made in the strategic process with each targeted donor, and are there at least twenty prospects being *actively* managed at any one time? How many gift targets have been realized over an eighteen-month period from those researched and rated as major donor prospects?

This kind of ongoing progress, as well as actual major gifts realized from established donors, should be part of the evaluation of the fundraiser's performance. Gift potential of the prospect pool, whatever its size, and the level of readiness of those prospects to make gifts must be considered among the standards for evaluating major gift success.

## Professional evaluation and expectation

Professional major gift fundraisers impose on themselves the most important evaluation and expectation. All the successful major gift fundraisers I know have higher expectations of themselves than does anyone else. They never seem to be satisfied with their own performance and continue to function in an unfinished-business mode. The mind-set they possess and the values and characteristics that drive them are their ultimate benchmark over time. They know that they, along with their major gift fundraising colleagues, are engaged in causes that are going to make the world a better place. They believe the adage that what you do for yourself dies with you, but what you do for others lives on. This motivates them at the highest level.

For the fundraiser, the final chapter in the major gift saga always relates to the donor. For them, the relationships and bonding that take place are life-changing and enormously satisfying. Although the relationship with the donor belongs to the organization and not to the major gift fundraiser, the shared experience of being part of a wonderful philanthropic act changes the life of the donor, the fundraiser, the beneficiary, and the organization forever. This truism is best expressed in the words of Winston Churchill: "We make a living by what we get, but we make a life by what we give."

ERNEST W. WOOD *is president of Ernest W. Wood & Company, Consultants in Philanthropy, a firm providing counsel in all aspects of fundraising, with an emphasis on major gifts and capital campaigns.*

*Integrating intradevelopment office initiatives, such as annual funds, planned giving, and capital campaigns, with major gift programs can dramatically increase fundraising results. These examples from university fundraising programs also apply to other development organizations.*

# 2

# Meshing development efforts with major gift fundraising

*Jerry A. May*

INCREASINGLY, development programs are becoming a complex set of highly specialized and sometimes independent fundraising efforts: annual giving, planned giving, corporate and foundation relations, constituency programs, capital campaigns, alumni relations, reunion giving, and major gift efforts. In some organizations these programs have become so focused, systematic, and professional that they are closer to science than art. The efforts are effective as specialties, but separateness and independence can lead to isolation, lost opportunity, organizational dysfunction, high staff turnover, lack of teamwork, and inefficiency. However, *specialization does not have to lead to compartmentalization.* Rather, an integrated series of fundraising efforts, linked to major gift work, can lead to more efficiency, greater productivity, deeper volunteer involvement, engaged and generous donors, and much more private support for the institution.

NEW DIRECTIONS FOR PHILANTHROPIC FUNDRAISING, NO. 16, SUMMER 1997 © JOSSEY-BASS PUBLISHERS

Where does one start when thinking about intradevelopment office issues and linkages? This chapter offers some principles and values of fundraising and major gift work.

## Centrality of major gifts

One of the truths about fundraising that experienced development professionals have known for at least two decades is that major gift fundraising (generally defined as obtaining commitments of a minimum of $50,000 to $100,000) brings in significantly more dollars to an organization than other fundraising initiatives. "Universities with a 10-year history of major gift efforts commonly find that 95 percent of their gift total comes from 5 percent or less of their donor base," according to Richard Matheny (1994, p. 11). Recent megacampaigns at Vanderbilt, Dartmouth, Ohio State, Michigan, and other schools illustrate these enormous major gift proportions.

## Significance of donor involvement

Another fundraising principle related to intradevelopment office issues is that the key element involved in motivating major gifts is the donor's personal involvement with the organization. Fundraisers refer to this donor involvement as *cultivation*, of course with the goal being to engage the donor. My favorite test of donor involvement is whether they refer to the organization in terms of "we" or "us" rather than "you" or "them."

One of the most common forms of involvement is serving as a volunteer on behalf of an organization: helping to raise money, promoting the organization, recruiting and persuading others to become involved, sitting on advisory boards and committees, knowing about the needs of the organization, and so on. The significance of volunteering and involvement is no mystery; it leads to commitment, which in turn leads to major gifts. A survey conducted by

INDEPENDENT SECTOR showed conclusively that "the incidence of volunteering has a direct relationship to the amount of contributions. The percentage of income contributed increases directly with the number of hours volunteered" (Matheny, 1994, p. 10).

## Fundamental importance of strong relationships with donors

Acquiring donors requires great effort and investment by development officers, organization leaders, and volunteers. The principal effort, of course, is obtaining initial access to a prospect and getting his or her attention, with the goal of developing a relationship that leads to involvement, engagement, and commitment. As Karen Osborne observes, donors do not have a relationship with an organization; they may identify with an organization, but they have relationships with people in the organization (Matheny, 1994).

One of the oldest axioms in fundraising is that people give to people. However, experienced fundraisers have learned a much more profound principle: the relationship between donors and people associated with the organization becomes the glue that bonds donors with an organization; often, it is part of the reason donors want to get more involved. The spirit of growing and expanding relationships is a powerful and captivating force in any major gift program.

Prior to developing those key relationships, however, major gift officers encounter some or all of the following responses: "I don't have time for you." "I haven't heard from your organization in years." "My family and I are committed to a huge set of our own priorities." "I really don't know anyone at your institution any more, and I am not interested." Good development officers are, of course, not deterred by this rejection. Their response is to develop a long sequence of steps in relationship building that often takes years before a major gift is realized.

However, there are strategic elements of the "relationship principle" that deserve to be further segmented and that are instructive when meshing other development efforts with major gift work. These strategic elements have been refined as the result of extensive contact and experience with potential donors.

## Maintaining continuous relationships with donors

Just as corporations spend a great deal to acquire customers and develop customer loyalty, so do the most successful fundraising organizations. These organizations systematically develop relationships with donors or prospective donors early in their careers and then keep and invest in those relationships, cultivating loyalty throughout the donors' lives.

## Developing relationships with the donor's family and friends

For decades, major gift decisions were made in large measure by the male head of a patriarchal family unit. Although some organizations astutely observed that widowed women were capable of major gifts, wives were often left out of the relationship-building process and gift discussions with the husband of the family. This, of course, was the reason why many gift discussions carried on for years remained unsuccessful: a left-out partner often vetoed a decision. As social values have evolved, so have the people making and influencing major gift decisions. In recent decades, the number of women working in professional positions has increased and family assets and family decisions about major gifts have become more shared.

The most professional and mature fundraising organizations do not stop at developing continuous relationships with husbands and wives, or significant partners. They extend the relationship in all directions to key family members (brothers, sisters, children, and even grandchildren) and key friends with whom a relationship can also be built. There are at least three important outcomes of this strategy. First, major gift decisions are more easily encouraged by influential family members and friends who have been brought under an organization's tent and who have been nurtured or treated with respect by the organization. The opposite, of course, is that sometimes it only takes one influential family member or close friend to object to a donor's major gift decision and stop, or at least inhibit, the decision process. Second, assets are often jointly held or linked in some way with private corporations, trusts, family foundations, or anticipated inheritances requiring joint support, approval, or consensus. Third, other family members and friends often become major donors themselves, stimulated by major gifts made by parents, siblings, or friends.

## Maintaining multiple relationships with donors

We know from experience that presidents, directors, and organization leaders often share their visions with donors, and this can become a motivating force in a major gift decision. Larry Wilson of Wilson Learning Associates supports this point when he notes that "people give to a vision rather than a need" (Matheny, 1994, p. 12). Hence, a relationship between a donor and someone with vision is enormously helpful, and often essential. But relationships should not stop here. In a fast-paced and competitive fundraising environment, a donor relationship involving a single individual in the organization puts major gifts at significant risk. Presidents and vice presidents come and go, and development officers move around as they climb development office ladders. Therefore, development organizations that encourage multiple relationships with donors have a better chance of providing continuous relationships and retaining donor loyalty over time. In addition, several people also can move along the cultivation process and possibly a major gift decision faster through more regular attention and intensive donor contact.

A third reason multiple relationships are of strategic importance is that several people can expose donors to more parts of the organization and thus stimulate more opportunities to give. Ultimately, the donor's potential to give grows much more over time.

## Linking other development programs with major gift efforts

One might rightfully ask why are we concerned with integrating the various fundraising specialities with major gift work. Why should we be concerned with the separateness and isolation of individual programs when they are raising a fair amount of money, when staff like having their "own" programs, and everything appears successful? The answer has at least three aspects. First, the whole of the development program is greater than the sum of its parts. Second, the results of major gift efforts are so enormous that all programs should feed into major gift activities to maximize results. Third, the principles identified in the foregoing discussion are underapplied when various development program areas do not cooperate in a unified lifetime process of working with donors. David Dunlop (1993) refers to this need for linkage of development program areas as the value of interdependence.

Let us look at linkage and interdependence and review how an interactive development program can maximize the results of major gift fundraising and ultimately the development program as a whole. We must keep in mind the preceding principles of relationships and involvement, further illuminated by Matheny's comment that to increase large gifts requires "an intensive donor contact strategy" (1994, p. 11). We must also consider Tom Broce's reflection that the process of involvement of donors and volunteers is no small investment for a fundraising program: "The meaningful involvement of individuals is a full-time never-ending task. It must be sincere, it must be constant, it must be real" (1979, p. 23).

### Annual giving

We know from experience that annual fund solicitations are often the first interface donors have at an organization with philanthropy and the practice of giving. First impressions and customer treatment are critical. "A successful major gift program cannot exist in isolation. . . . Annual giving is the primary avenue by which donors come to include a college or university in their giving plans. If the annual giving program treats prospective donors badly, they will be unlikely to maintain or increase their giving" (Cosovich, 1993, p. 3). Clearly then, the treatment of annual giving donors is the first way an annual giving program is linked to a major gift program. The development of donor loyalty is fundamental.

Annual giving performs other functions that later have an impact on major gift prospects. These include regularity of contact, the beginning of a giving relationship, how a donor is thanked personally, and how quickly the gift receipt is sent out. Each of these factors builds a relationship for a major gift program.

Another annual giving linkage is the expectation and process of upgrading an annual donor. This is what gets the major gift process started for many donors. "Donors who have upgraded in gift level on a consistent basis have demonstrated their loyalty to, and enthusiasm for, the mission. These donors have qualified themselves to be willing and perhaps capable of considering a major gift" (Matheny, 1994, p. 4). Programs that do not aggressively and tastefully condition donors for upgraded gifts are not supporting the major gift efforts to come later—and are actually conditioning donors to think small. Donor recognition levels and activities are, of course, one of the principal vehicles some annual giving programs use to thank donors and cultivate them for the future.

Perhaps the most substantial way annual giving programs can link with and support major gift activity is by furthering the principle of involvement. Annual fund volunteer committees, class gift and reunion volunteer committees, parents' fund volunteer committees, friends volunteer committees, annual giving chairs, and regional chairs all serve to increase donor commitment. However, when the volunteers are selected for not only their enthusiasm but also their potential as major gift donors either in the near term or in the future, the annual giving program begins to develop an almost seamless linkage with major gift efforts. The principle of strategically involving and placing (adult) children and friends of major donor prospects on committees and developing relationships with them enhances the family's commitment to the university and support for major gifts down the road.

Annual giving staff raise money for the organization each year (while focusing on increasing annual support), develop loyalty for lifetime partnerships with donors, and cultivate donors through contact and involvement for major gifts.

### Corporate and foundation relations

Although we know that corporations are regularly cultivated and asked for annual and major gifts, organizations do not uniformly develop a strategic relationship between a corporate fundraising program and the individual-giving side of a major gift effort.

Once again, operating under principles of contact, involvement, and relationship building, corporate fundraising programs can identify successful executives to become involved with organizations and focus on common issues and needs. Corporate programs can also involve constituents inside corporations at all levels in annual giving solicitations, drawing on a linkage with the annual giving program and using corporate matching gifts as further incentive for participation.

Corporate relations programs can best support major gift efforts by supporting the growth of corporate advisory committees. It can be enormously fruitful to place major donor prospects strategically on committees established to receive meaningful advice on fundraising, financial or investment issues, faculty development issues, and corporate-organization partnership issues. Some organizations avoid such linkages for fear of corporate interference in the organization; the best measure of protection is not to avoid such interaction, but rather to have a thoughtful set of guidelines for the objectives and roles of such advisory committees.

Clearly this kind of corporate involvement can further relationships and increase the likelihood of corporate and individual major gifts.

### Planned giving

Of the different development program areas, planned giving is generally most closely associated with major gifts in terms of interdependence, or at least linkage. Planned giving prospects are often major gift prospects. Indeed, Northwestern University has recognized this linkage so formally in its organization that the regional major gift staff and planned giving staff are one entity, trained in both fundraising methodologies.

However, there are other strategic actions that planned giving programs can bring to major gift efforts. Planned giving donors who are major gift prospects, or whose families and friends are major gift prospects, can be featured in planned giving publications and receive some formal recognition as planned giving donors. This can further serve to engage the planned giving donor and ease him or her into a position to provide a major lifetime gift.

Planned giving programs can also develop volunteers to host events for planned giving prospects, sponsor planned giving seminars, or help solicit individual planned gifts in partnership with planned giving professionals. The involvement of these volunteers can lead to both planned and major gifts from the volunteers and other donors brought closer through these activities.

Planned giving programs can also have a more intentional link with annual giving programs that lead to large gifts over time. Many development offices are personally familiar with an anecdotal regular donor who gave $40 a year for thirty years and passed away, leaving a surprising gift of $1 million. Planned giving programs that tastefully market to longtime annual donors more intentionally and systematically can make these isolated anecdotes a common occurrence.

Of course, the planned giving link to capital campaigns is readily apparent, but it is implemented differently across the development landscape. Some organizations, in their focus on cash gifts, have left planned giving out of campaign goals, as some have done with annual giving as well. Many organizations have integrated planned giving into campaigns and discounted the gifts based on actuarial age. More recently, several universities—Michigan, Vanderbilt, Ohio State, and Illinois—have devised separate goals for planned gifts alongside the cash gift goals to highlight the importance of both.

Whatever the case, planned giving is more than ever an interdependent part of capital campaigns and an effort that feeds major gifts. Many organizations are finding that structuring a major gift with a trust or bequest component significantly enhances a donor's motivation for a very large campaign gift.

Recent campaign results at Vanderbilt, Illinois, Michigan, Ohio State, and Yale (campaigns ranging from $500 million to $1.5 billion) have planned revocable and irrevocable gifts totaling 15–32 percent of campaign totals. The significance of this is that the partnership between planned giving and major gifts is key, because approximately 95 percent of campaign totals are from major gifts.

### Capital campaigns: Building momentum and stimulating major gifts

The interdependence and interrelationship between major gifts and capital campaigns are the most highly developed, except where inexperienced development staff or others think that a campaign can be successful by securing modest-sized gifts from 100 percent of the constituents. This naïve point of view generally receives a silent and collective groan from seasoned development officers. Experience has proven that public universities, for instance, are fortunate to get a 20 percent participation rate in campaigns (30–60 percent among most private colleges and universities)—even after fundraising has had decades to become accepted.

Campaigns provide major donor prospects with highly motivating factors: a clear and substantial set of goals, a vision for the future of the organization, a time frame for making commitments, and a volunteer organization to enhance involvement and relationships. As Dunlop says, "Capital campaigns are another example of how nurturing fundraising depends on the work of others in the development office. The urgency of campaign fundraising often captures the attention of some of the institution's best prospects" (1993, p. 13).

One of the great motivators for major donors during campaigns is that the organization is trying to do more than grow incrementally; the appeal lies in the leap strategy that the campaign represents, the challenge to take the university to a much higher level of financial support, quality, and opportunity in a relatively short period of time.

### Precampaign

Veterans of major campaigns have learned that in order to stimulate major gifts, planning and implementation are the keys to building momentum and establishing an environment in which people give (or at least expect to be asked to give) large gifts. Matheny (1994) talks about the importance of involving volunteer leadership before a campaign or major gift effort takes place. This helps share ownership, create expectations, and build momentum. One of the most common techniques of this precampaign period is the "leadership gifts," or "nucleus fund," phase. This effort relies in large part on major gifts and serves to provide a deadline and some urgency to create campaign momentum.

Intradevelopment office units can best support major gift activities during this precampaign period by bringing groups of volunteers, many of them major gift prospects, to the planning teams for each component of the campaign. Early partnership yields some good ideas, thoughtful strategies, and deeper relationships and involvement.

### Campaign

Creating and maintaining momentum during a campaign also requires a team effort by all units of an integrated development program. Among the most common vehicles for creating momentum are the following:

- A major, high-visibility campaign kickoff, featuring major gift leadership.
- A series of campaign events or regional kickoff events at home and across the areas where prospects, particularly major donor prospects, are located.
- A series of publications and communication features that identify the needs of the campaign, coming out of all areas of the

28

development program. It is essential to list substantial naming-gift opportunities targeted to major gift donors.

- Steady and systematic announcement of lead gifts and major gifts, targeted to different regions, constituencies, and prospect groups.
- Ongoing recruitment and meeting of volunteers for all development programs, once again with a focus on bringing major gift prospects under the campaign umbrella and into deeper involvement.
- Regular communication throughout the campaign highlighting the impact of donors to different development programs and campaign components. Perhaps the biggest shortcoming of many campaigns is the failure to report broadly and often about the impact of all gifts, especially major gifts.
- Periodic celebration during the campaign to show accomplishment and maintain momentum.

### Postcampaign

Continuing momentum for major gifts in the postcampaign period is generally one of the most difficult assignments to accomplish. This is a time when major gift donors are often still paying off pledges and are sometimes seeking some relief from the long campaign.

One operating principle is essential during this period: *make all donors in all programs feel successful, proud, and well-thanked!*

The glow of a campaign is a key to the future for repeat donors and increasingly large major gifts. In addition, several postcampaign strategies can be implemented:

- Continue to feature current needs from individual components of the campaign. There are often areas within the overall goal that fall short.
- Continue to pursue major gift prospects who were discovered in the later stages of the campaign but not involved or committed enough to make a substantial contribution.
- Pursue major gift donors who paid pledges early and still have the capacity to give substantially more support.

- Provide focused stewardship programs thanking many major donors and showing them the impact of their gifts (stewardship itself often stimulates a recurring major gift during this period, or at least prepares the way for a new ask to a donor).
- Develop minicampaigns at the end of the campaign for a new building or a special endowment or program goal to generate new excitement.
- Conduct postcampaign planning with organization leaders and volunteers to look at other areas for ongoing support during the postcampaign period.
- Thank campaign volunteers for their service, and bring in new volunteers to mix with the seasoned volunteers whose commitment has not waned.

### *References*

Broce, T. E. *Fundraising: The Guide to Raising Money from Private Sources.* Norman: University of Oklahoma Press, 1979.

Cosovich, J. "An Introduction to the Major Gift Process." In R. Muir and J. May (eds.), *Developing an Effective Major Gift Program: From Managing Staff to Soliciting Gifts.* Washington, D.C.: Council for Advancement and Support of Education, 1993.

Dunlop, D. R. "Strategic Management of a Major Gift Program." In R. Muir and J. May (eds.), *Developing an Effective Major Gift Program: From Managing Staff to Soliciting Gifts.* Washington, D.C.: Council for Advancement and Support of Education, 1993.

Matheny, R. E. *Major Gifts Solicitation Strategies.* Washington, D.C.: Council for Advancement and Support of Education, 1994.

JERRY A. MAY *is vice president for development at Ohio State University.*

*Having a framework for managing an institution's major gifts program is probably the most important component of a successful development program. The cultivation process and the moves management philosophy are outlined and detailed for immediate implementation.*

# 3

# Managing a successful major gifts program

*Paul B. Smith*

ALTHOUGH MOST OF US RECOGNIZE the importance of major gifts to our institutions, we do not spend the time or allocate the resources necessary to be highly successful in securing major gift support. With over 90 percent of the funds normally given to non-profit institutions coming from fewer than 5 percent of the total donors, it is not surprising that the importance of major gifts has never been more significant.

What is needed is a systematic method for cultivating and nurturing relationships with potential donors who have the ability to make such important contributions. This process can be applied to development operations of any size, from the one-person office to a multilevel office with staff for various tiers of donors.

NEW DIRECTIONS FOR PHILANTHROPIC FUNDRAISING, NO. 16, SUMMER 1997 © JOSSEY-BASS PUBLISHERS

### *The cultivation cycle and moves management theory*

The cultivation cycle is a model of how relationships develop for all of us. It therefore follows that in securing major gifts *we need to be concerned primarily with caring and nurturing a strong relationship with our donors,* and less concerned with securing an immediate commitment. This is not to say that securing a gift is not important. But if we genuinely care for the hopes, dreams, and aspirations of our donors, they will desire to make a significant investment. *The significance of the gift for the donor is what is most important,* as opposed to its significance to the institution.

In the early 1960s, G. T. "Buck" Smith was vice president of the College of Wooster in Wooster, Ohio. He started his development career at Cornell University. While traveling the back roads of rural Ohio visiting alumni and friends of Wooster, Buck developed the ideas that have become known as the cultivation cycle and the moves management system.

The cultivation of potentially large donors should be as systematic and continuing an effort as possible. The cultivation cycle involves five steps, all of which begin with the letter *I*:

1. Identification
2. Information
3. Interest
4. Involvement
5. Investment

The (1) *identification* of possible donors should only occur once. It is a two-way street: we identify a donor and the donor identifies us. The final four steps make up a continuing cycle of (2) learning additional *information* about the potential donor, (3) furthering his or her *interest* in the institution or cause, (4) encouraging meaningful *involvement* in at least one phase of the institution or program, and ultimately (5) receiving his or her *investment.*

The moves management theory came out of the idea of the cultivation cycle; it puts into place a system of initiatives that "move" an individual through the cycle and further a potential donor's relationship to the point of investment. A *move* is defined as meaningful engagement of or interaction with a potential donor. It involves a penetration of his or her consciousness that is intentional and planned. The idea of moves is not, as some have thought, making manipulative actions to get a person to make a commitment. Rather, moves emphasize nurturing and fostering a passion in an individual to want to make a significant difference in an institution, program, or cause that can bring the potential donor great joy and satisfaction.

## Implementing the moves management system

Given the importance of major gifts to the overall success of any development program, it follows that the chief executive and members of the board of trustees, particularly members of the development committee, need to embrace the philosophy of cultivation of donors and help promote a development ethos or culture that fosters the building of meaningful relationships with donors.

In order to keep track of initiatives with prospective donors and to create accountability with all staff members, a structure needs to be put in place. The chief development officer of an institution must be the primary cultivator, assuming responsibility for the management of prospects. In some situations, it may be appropriate and feasible to have one staff member designated the *moves manager*, to oversee tracking of moves and to keep other staff members focused on developing and implementing cultivation strategies with prospects.

There are six basic steps in facilitating the cultivation process.

First, a list of all known potential major donors needs to be compiled with as much information as is readily available on each. This is a list that will never be "complete" because additional names are identified and added over time. The term *major gift* deserves some clarification. An institution needs to determine what a major gift is based upon the level of support the institution requires. One good way to determine the major gift level is to look at the highest category of gifts for annual support and make this the floor for a major gift designation. For example, if the highest giving to an annual fund is $10,000, major gift donors will be cultivated for gifts of $10,000 and greater. Gifts above this threshold can then be broken into additional categories, such as special ($10,000–100,000), major ($100,000 to $1 million) and leadership ($1 million and up).

Second, each prospective donor should then be "classified" based upon estimated capacity to give and readiness to give. *Capacity* to give is a prospect's gift potential, not the amount of the gift being sought or what we expect his or her next gift to be. Capacity is determined by research, either through public sources of information or by information gained from others who know a prospect's giving capacity either directly or indirectly. *Readiness* is a subjective measurement of how developed the relationship is with a prospect and whether an individual is ready to consider making a major commitment and investment.

Capacity to give can be designated with five classifications:

1    $1 million and up
2    $100,000–$1 million
3    $25,000–$100,000
4    $1,000–$25,000
9    To be determined

Similarly, readiness to give is identified using five categories:

A    Ready to invest (or reinvest)
B    Needs some cultivation
C    Needs extensive cultivation
D    Has marginal interest
U    To be determined

Within each classification, potential donors need to be prioritized based on their gift capacity and readiness to give (for example, all those with a 1-A classification, 1-B, 1-C, 1-D, 2-A, etc.).

Third, once the list has been sorted by classification, a priority code is assigned to each prospect. Priority codes refer to the number of initiatives, contacts, or moves that a prospect requires in a year. Development or major gift officers spending 60–80 percent of their time on the cultivation of major donor prospects can normally manage up to one hundred prospects. Of this one hundred, roughly 10 percent, or the top ten prospects, should probably have a minimum of twelve cultivation moves per year, or one move per month. These top ten individuals would be given a priority code of 1.

The next twenty prospects should receive six to eight moves per year, or basically bimonthly contact. These prospective donors are given a priority 2 code. The next thirty prospects should receive four or five moves per year, or quarterly contact. They are given a priority code of 3. The remaining forty prospects should receive two or three moves per year, or semiannual contact. They are given a code of 4. In rare instances, a prospect may only require annual contact (code 5), but such an individual is not a serious major gift prospect and should not be kept on the list.

With this breakdown of contacts with one hundred prospects, a major gifts officer makes over 450 moves per year. In actual practice, this number usually approaches six hundred moves with the volume of activity generated with one hundred prospects. This requires that four or five moves be made each day, assuming four out of five days each week are spent on active cultivation of prospective major gift donors.

The fourth facilitating step is to start with the top ten prospects and then continue through the entire prospect list, developing a cultivation plan or strategy for each potential donor with an initial six-month schedule outlined for each. A cultivation strategy is a plan of action designed to further the relationship of an individual with an institution in such a way that the person's interest (the third step in the cultivation cycle) is heightened and greater involvement (fourth step) is encouraged, which leads to an investment (fifth step) in something the person cares about deeply.

The process of nurturing and developing such relationships must be done with careful planning. The specific needs and interests of a particular prospective donor must be examined to determine the most natural and appropriate course of action to pursue. The key research needed to know these most personal things must usually come from direct contact with the prospect or from information given by close friends or associates. Initial steps of cultivation may involve meeting with prospective donors at their homes or places of business, with the expressed desire to thank them for past support or involvement and to come to know them better. Much can be learned by asking individuals who are already supporting an institution about people they know, or about individuals the development office has identified whom they might know.

Once information has been learned about a person's interests, a plan can be developed to involve that individual in the life of the institution to further his or her interest and commitment to a specific project or program. The role of volunteers is especially important in this stage of cultivation. It is far more difficult to get an appointment than it is to get a gift. The first introduction to a person is often the most critical, especially if it can be made by a person with whom the prospect has confidence and trust.

It is important that donors be sufficiently involved in the life of the institution before moving them from a position of knowledge or initial interest to the investment stage of the relationship. Of course, in unique situations, a person can move quickly from having an initial interest in a cause to making a major investment. However, the general rule is that people need to become involved in a cause or institution before they are ready to consider a "sacrificial" commitment.

Remember, a major gift is something that is major to a donor: a gift that requires thought and reflection, often to the point of giving up something in order to take advantage of a philanthropic opportunity. All individuals must make choices with their resources. We support causes whose mission we embrace, in whose leadership (including trustees, staff, and key volunteers) we have confidence, and whose financial footing is sound.

Once people's interests have been determined and they have been sufficiently involved in the life of an institution, an *invitation* should be designed to encourage their investment. In keeping with our desire to relate sensitively with our prospective donors, we want to invite their investment and participation with our institution. The difference between an invitation and a proposal is one of relationship. Among individuals with whom we have a close personal relationship, it is more appropriate to extend an invitation for them to join us rather than sending a proposal. The words we use to seek major gift support are as important as the thoughtfulness with which we approach each cultivation move.

Fifth, as part of the process of developing a cultivation strategy for a prospective major gift donor, primary (and in some instances secondary) responsibility for managing the cultivation needs to be assigned to a staff person or key volunteer. Generally, the primary responsibility should be given to a staff member who then serves as the point person, coordinating all activities with the donor and being responsible for monitoring the progress of a particular strategy. The "primary" might be the staff person within the organization who has the closest and most natural relationship with a prospect.

There is often at least one other individual who has a close relationship with a prospective donor; this person should be assigned secondary status as a cultivator and resource. If this person is a volunteer, we often call him or her a "natural partner." The secondary or natural partner needs to be consulted whenever a strategy is being developed or modified so that advice and counsel can be given, in addition to participating in the cultivation initiatives as a friendly advocate for the institution. A side benefit to involving volunteers and other close friends in this process is that this participation serves as a natural and affirming means of further involvement for the secondary partner.

One rule is especially important when involving volunteers: it must be made clear we will never ask volunteers to do anything that makes them feel uncomfortable. Only in an environment of mutual trust and respect can we hope to deepen the relationships for long-term benefit to the institution. Little can be gained by pushing for short-term results that have long-lasting negative effects.

The sixth and final step in the implementation of the cultivation cycle and moves management system involves maintaining accountability of all staff members and volunteers involved in the process of nurturing and securing major gift support. It has been our experience that formation of a *major gifts task force*, made up of anyone with primary responsibility for the cultivation of major gift donors, is vital to implementing the process. One person, usually the chief development officer or the individual responsible for major gifts, serves as the chair of the task force.

The major gifts task force (MGTF) should meet at a regularly scheduled time, preferably once every two weeks but no less frequently than once a month. The purpose of this meeting is to review cultivation moves that have taken place, and most importantly plan future cultivation moves for each person's major gift prospects. All members should spend time prior to the MGTF meeting writing their own thoughts on cultivation of key prospects, which can be shared with other members for their input. The value of meeting as a group comes from the shared information and team approach to developing meaningful strategies based upon the collective knowledge of the members.

The chair of the MGTF, or moves manager, is responsible for keeping the other members accountable for the moves they plan to make and for coordinating the moves. If possible, minutes should be taken at these meetings and a summary distributed to the members of the MGTF within twenty-four hours of the meeting for quick follow-up. There are three reporting forms that help facilitate the management of the system: a *call report*, a *cultivation summary*, and a *cultivation schedule* for tracking moves made and planned.

The call report is something that each person in the cultivation process keeps close at hand (Exhibit 3.1). It should be filled out as soon as possible after a meaningful contact with an individual or prospective donor, whether by telephone call or personal visit. Any information gained from the contact that helps to further the information known about an individual or their interests should be noted. A plan of action for the next move is noted along with any

**Exhibit 3.1. Call report**

Contact date: _____

Submitted by: _____

Circle one:          Personal visit          Phone call          Letter

Person(s) contacted: _____

Contact summary: _____

_____

Contact details: _____

_____

_____

_____

_____

_____

_____

_____

Next moves:

(1) _____

(2) _____

(3) _____

follow-up items and specific completion dates. Copies of any correspondence should be attached and entered into the cultivation schedule.

The cultivation summary is a two-page form, designed within a database system or used on its own, that summarizes the information known about a person on the first page (personal data, outside interests, interests at the institution, past and present involvement, giving history). It outlines the moves strategy for cultivating the donor's relationship with the institution on the second page (Exhibit 3.2). In order to develop meaningful initiatives, a long-term goal

**Exhibit 3.2. Cultivation summary**

```
        2
        |
        |    3
     ___|___
    /       \
1 --|         |
    \       /
   5 ---___---  4
```

Date prepared: _____
Classification: _____
Mail code: _____
Primary/secondary
  responsibility: _____

1. Identification

Name: _____
Home address: _____
City: _____ State: _____ Zip: _____
Home phone: _____

Business name: _____
Business address: _____ Title: _____
City: _____ State: _____ Zip: _____
Business phone: _____ Fax: _____

2. Information

Birthdate: _____ School: _____ Year: _____
Spouse: _____ School: _____ Year: _____
Family 1: _____ School: _____ Year: _____
Family 2: _____ School: _____ Year: _____
Family 3: _____ School: _____ Year: _____

General remarks:

3. Interests

   Religious, cultural, civic, political:
   At your institution:

4. Involvement

   Past:
   Potential:
   Known well by:

5. Investment

   *Past gifts:* (Most recent listed first)

   | | | | *Gift potential:* |
   |---|---|---|---|
   | Date: _____ | Amt: $ _____ | For: _____ | Annual: _____ |
   | Date: _____ | Amt: $ _____ | For: _____ | Capital: _____ |
   | Date: _____ | Amt: $ _____ | For: _____ | Estate: _____ |
   | Date: _____ | Amt: $ _____ | For: _____ | Other: _____ |
   | Date: _____ | Amt: $ _____ | For: _____ | |

   *Outstanding pledges:*

   | | | | *Gift level:* |
   |---|---|---|---|
   | Date: _____ | Amt: $ _____ | For: _____ | Gift club: _____ |
   | Date: _____ | Amt: $ _____ | For: _____ | "     ": _____ |
   | Date: _____ | Amt: $ _____ | For: _____ | "     ": _____ |
   | Date: _____ | Amt: $ _____ | For: _____ | Yrs. consecutive: _____ |

**Exhibit 3.2.** (*continued*)

Cultivation Plan and Response Record

Prospect: _____

(For visits or phone contacts, list persons involved, location, and subjects discussed. For proposals, list amount requested, purpose, project director if applicable, and outcome.)

1. Date:
   Activity:
   Reaction or outcome:

2. Date:
   Activity:
   Reaction or outcome:

3. Date:
   Activity:
   Reaction or outcome:

needs to be articulated, as well as a short-term strategy upon which to base the moves. It is important to note who is responsible for carrying out the move and the target date for completion.

Once a contact has been made, the result should be noted and the next cultivation step detailed. The contacts from the call reports should be summarized in the donor's record for review by other staff members. Circulate these summaries weekly to all staff members involved in the cultivation of major gift donors, so everyone is aware of initiatives taken and planned.

The cultivation schedule uses the information in the call report and cultivation summary to track the moves completed and, importantly, show the planned initiatives for a prospect (Exhibit 3.3). This management tool can keep track of a large number of prospects, providing a snapshot of activity at a glance.

The cultivation schedule uses a spreadsheet format, so that the form can be sorted on any of the fields. The first column is for the priority codes, signifying the frequency of contacts needed as described above. The name field is entered with the last name first, followed by the first name of the prospect and spouse. The year field is for the year of graduation and any other affiliations (such as *T* for a current trustee, *FT* for a former trustee, *P* for parent, *Gp* for grandparent, etc.). The CS field is to be checked if a cultivation summary has been completed on the prospect. The two classification fields are for the capacity and readiness codes. The person assigned primary responsibility is noted in the Prim. field, as is the secondary partner in the Sec. field. The Reg. field can be used to note the primary location of a prospect (state, region, or city). "Proj." stands for project and can be used to note a particular interest on the part of the prospect (for example, scholarship endowment, building program, special program). The GO field signifies a gift objective for a possible next gift. This should only be used when the cultivation process has progressed enough to have a good sense of the possible gift range a prospect is likely to consider for a particular project. It should be left blank until a reasonable and realistic estimate can be made.

# Exhibit 3.3. Cultivation schedule

Date prepared:

**Priority Codes:**
1 = Monthly contact
2 = Bimonthly contact
3 = Quarterly contact
4 = Semiannual contact
5 = Annual contact

**Classification Codes:**
1 = $1 million and up
2 = $100,000–$1 million
3 = $25,000–$100,000
4 = $1,000–$25,000
9 = To be determined

A = Ready to invest
B = Needs some cultivation
C = Needs extensive cultivation
D = Has marginal interest
U = To be determined

**Types of Contacts:**
L = Letter
T = Telephone call
P = Personal visit
(Uppercase = Completed action)
(Lowercase = Planned/anticipated action)

| P | Name | Year | CS | Class | Prim. | Sec. | Reg. | Proj. | GO | January | | | | February | | | | March | | | | April | | | | May | | | | June | | |
|---|---|---|---|---|---|---|---|---|---|---|---|---|---|---|---|---|---|---|---|---|---|---|---|---|---|---|---|---|---|---|---|---|
| | | | | | | | | | | 1 | 8 | 15 | 22 | 29 | 5 | 12 | 19 | 26 | 4 | 11 | 18 | 25 | 1 | 8 | 15 | 22 | 29 | 6 | 13 | 20 | 27 | 3 | 10 | 17 | 24 |

# Cultivation Information

| Home Address | City | State | Zip | Home Phone | Business Phone | COMMENTS |
|---|---|---|---|---|---|---|
| | | | | | | |
| | | | | | | |
| | | | | | | |
| | | | | | | |
| | | | | | | |
| | | | | | | |
| | | | | | | |
| | | | | | | |
| | | | | | | |
| | | | | | | |
| | | | | | | |
| | | | | | | |
| | | | | | | |
| | | | | | | |
| | | | | | | |
| | | | | | | |

The remaining portion of the cultivation schedule is a rolling calendar for keeping track of the moves. The different types of contacts are filled in for the respective weeks of completed or planned activity. A completed action is noted in uppercase, while a planned action is noted in lowercase. Any contact or initiative that results in the prospect's consciousness being meaningfully raised should be noted.

The moves manager is responsible for seeing that contacts are filled in consistently and that other MGTF members are held accountable for filling in the cultivation schedule regularly (weekly if possible) and for planning future initiatives. It may be useful to create a special notebook, to be kept by each MGTF member, that includes the list of prospects each is responsible for, a complete list of the major donors in the cultivation schedule, copies of cultivation summaries on a member's top prospects, copies of minutes from MGTF meetings, and a supply of blank call reports.

---

## *Summary*

Securing the gift—the fifth, or investment, phase of the cultivation cycle—is the natural culmination of relationship building. It is through this act of giving that the donor and the institution are linked. By making a commitment, people give something of themselves that must be cared for and appreciated by others. Stewardship of a donor needs careful thought, with specific initiatives selected to have special meaning. This is in fact the continuation of the cultivation cycle, as a person gains greater involvement and desires to make an even greater investment.

A successful major gifts program, and development in general, is concerned with far more than just raising money. Those who spend their time nurturing relationships with people who have the capacity to make a real difference will realize huge results not only in dollars raised but in the number of people who care deeply about their institution and will support it for years to come.

PAUL B. SMITH *is president of Smith Associates Consulting and Management Group, a fundraising consulting firm founded by his father, G. T. "Buck" Smith. The firm specializes in providing counsel to colleges, universities, independent schools, and nonprofit institutions in all areas of development.*

*A manual on gift policy helps donors, volunteers, and staff avoid ethical pitfalls in prospect discovery, research, solicitation, and gift stewardship.*

# 4

# Ethics and major gifts

*Joseph S. Beyel*

*Ethics* ('e-thiks) npl: 1 the study of standards of conduct and moral judgment; moral philosophy 2 a treatise on this study 3 the system or code of morals of a particular person, religion, group, profession, etc.

*Gift* (gift) n: 1 something given to show friendship, affection, support, etc.; present 2 the act, power, or right of giving 3 a natural ability; talent

*Philanthropy* (fi-'lan-thro-pe) n: 1 a desire to help mankind, esp. as shown by gifts to charitable or humanitarian institutions; benevolence

WHY SHOULD WE EVEN be concerned about the conduct of our profession? In our work, we attempt to bring together the desires of our benefactors with the good outcomes their gifts may achieve. New cures, new advances in education, and the sustained good of many nonprofit organizations are all positive outcomes of philanthropy. However, a modern approach to the raising of funds is grounded in the reality of the modern world: invasive news-gathering media, enormous advances in communications, the desire for personal privacy, and an affluent society. These realities often collide in the pursuit of philanthropy.

NEW DIRECTIONS FOR PHILANTHROPIC FUNDRAISING, NO. 16, SUMMER 1997 © JOSSEY-BASS PUBLISHERS

There are few ethical dilemmas in major gift fundraising if we act as a diligent and ethical profession. These dilemmas usually involve prospect discovery, prospect research and solicitation, and gift stewardship.

The fundraising adage of 60/40—that is, 60 percent of philanthropic gifts coming from 40 percent of the donors—is true in many organizations. Major gifts are not common; they are made by only a few among our constituents. The search for and identification of these few donors is the first ethical dilemma we must consider.

In a presentation to a group of advancement professionals from academic medical centers (Association of American Medical Colleges, April 12, 1991), I used fictional case studies to engage the audience in identifying some of the ethical dilemmas of fundraising for major gifts. In this chapter, I use a couple of those fictional situations to develop the argument for each "ethical hurdle."

## Prospect identification: How do we find the few?

The most perplexing problem facing development professionals and their research colleagues is, "How do we identify our major gift prospects?" In an open forum discussion in the mid–1980s with Carl Cohen, professor of medical ethics at the University of Michigan, we debated the need to identify new potential donors and how that activity might be perceived by our patients. Among the questions Cohen posed: Could our patients perceive that they will receive better medical care if they made a philanthropic gift to our medical center? Could they feel medically threatened if they did not make a gift?

For me, the questions were shocking. I had never even considered both sides of the issue. Conceivably, the answers are yes and no. If a gift advances science and creates new opportunities for therapies or even cures, the answer is yes, care will be better. But if a patient considers that it's necessary to give a gift to receive "better" medical care, then the gift decision carries a perceived threat and the answer is no. There is a dilemma in balancing potential new therapies and cures versus threats and differing levels of health care delivery. How do we develop an ethical process that solves such ethical dilemmas?

The following case, which continues the doctor-patient relationship, might help us work through the analysis.

Patients come to hospitals and medical centers for many reasons and usually consider their personal health or sickness a private matter. Most patients consider it an invasion of privacy if nonmedical personnel are aware of their medical condition (diagnosis and prognosis) and their relationship with the medical institution. Also, physicians have a moral bond with their patients and are expected to treat the doctor-patient relationship confidentially.

What ethical analyses are made by the major gifts directors for a hospital or medical center? What routes do they take to increase the numbers of major gift prospects for their institutions? To answer, a well-structured set of rules or principles is necessary.

The decision tree or set of rules must begin with a study of the institution's mission, values, and moral philosophy; after all, a health care institution is a place where the sick are treated and (most often) healed. Academic medical centers care for the sick; educate generations of practitioners; and discover, through basic and clinical science research, new therapeutic and diagnostic tools to improve a society's health and well-being.

Practitioners and medical researchers focus on healing as the core of their mission. "First, do no harm!" is a fundamental guiding principle among health care practitioners. In creating a potential donor discovery system, one must answer Cohen's questions about the perceptions among patients. Will a philanthropic donor receive better care and a nondonor inferior care? In screening patients with an eye to discovering major gift donors, is it possible for the patient to be harmed? Gifts and philanthropy, as defined at the opening of the chapter, are transactions of friendship for the greater good of humanity.

In building a credible philanthropy program, fundraising professionals must acknowledge the need for external private support.

For us to find the few among a broad spectrum of constituents, an informed gift decision is required of our constituents—patients, alumni, community leaders, and others. The chance to help them help a charitable cause follows a process of informed consent, similar to the informed consent process in the doctor-patient relationship. In the philanthropic informed consent process, an institution identifies its strengths and weaknesses and its opportunities and threats. Philanthropic major gifts are realized after careful information gathering and after prospective donors have engaged with the institution over time. However, charitable organizations need the consent of their publics so that these mature relationships can happen. The act of informing constituents of the mission, values, and moral philosophy of the institution and its existence as a not-for-profit charitable organization increases their knowledge base. Sharing the goals and objectives of the organization deepens the relationship. The impact of donors' philanthropic support is an outcome of these matured relationships. Each constituent must be offered an opportunity to make an informed decision in a practical way.

Through philanthropic informed consent, the potential-donor discovery process develops as a moral and ethical engagement. The opinions of the best friends of an institution—alumni, staff, faculty, and current volunteers and donors—are an aid in sharing institutional information and support for the timing of the first philanthropic contact. The path of engagement might flow as follows:

- Share the institution's mission, statement of values, and moral philosophy with all constituents—clients, friends, community leaders, volunteer staff, and other appropriate groups.
- Share the organizational goals and objectives, including philanthropic objectives, with all constituents.
- Offer testimonials from current and former donors on the critical impact of their gift to the institution.
- Recognize the personal nature of philanthropy and that gifts, at all levels, secure the future of the organization.

- Ask for their partnership, as volunteers and donors in the institution.
- Be certain that each person has an option to say no.

Cohen may find fault that we have not resolved specifically the perceived threat of a conscious double standard of health care delivery in this pathway. However, in this sequence of informed consent it is crucial when and how the opportunity is presented. In a health care delivery setting, this could be at the time of first contact with a physician or other health care provider, in postvisit documents, or several months later. For college and university alumni, informed consent might begin with graduation day—or the first day of admission to the university! The right time is when thoughtful consideration can be given to this emotional relationship with the charitable nonprofit. Let your best friends help you.

## *Philanthropic research*

What and how much should we know in order to determine whether a constituent is a potential major gift donor?

Potential donor research is the backbone of a major gifts program. The fundraiser's judgment requires fact, not rumor or innuendo. Multiple avenues exist to examine the financial ability of potential donors, whether individual, corporate, or foundation. Corporation and foundation interest in supporting an organization is fairly straightforward. Such potential donors offer public information about their philanthropic interests. Corporations often develop contributions programs, and grant-making foundations are created for the purpose of distributing philanthropic grants and gifts. Identifying opportunities, levels of support, and inclinations to give are simple matters and rarely need an ethical examination. However, in forming a judgment about an individual, fundraisers often tread closely to the line of unethical practice. We cross the line when we gain personal and financial information apart from the public domain.

The fictional scenario that follows is exaggerated to illustrate this point.

A senior development officer has had phenomenal success for three years in assessing the financial condition of several little-known prospective donors. The information has been employed in developing solicitation strategies resulting in at least ten major gifts. The gift outcomes have been so impressive that she has been promoted and financially rewarded.

As the leader of the organization's development program, you get to know these new major donors and in time discover a common denominator among them. All of them share the same financial institution—the one employing your colleague's spouse in its private banking department. You investigate and discover the obvious. He supplied confidential financial information to his wife. Her judgments in creating solicitation strategies were fact-based, but the method of collection crossed the line of ethical practice.

An exaggeration? Probably. An ethical dilemma? Clearly!

Here are ethical questions that might be asked in such a situation:

- Do we tell our donors about our practice of prospective donor research?
- Do we tell about colleague's unethical behavior?
- Do we offer to return donors' philanthropic gifts resulting from this practice?
- Do we attempt to persuade our donors to continue their support?
- Do we dismiss the development officer from employment?
- Do we ask our donors and volunteers for advice on prospective donor research methods?

Is a gift something given to show friendship? Is a gift a desire to help humanity? Is ethics a system or a code of morals of a profession? The answer to each question is yes. The data we require to make a gift-capacity judgment can be found in the public record. Access to the public record allows one, practically and ethically, to collect sufficient information from county courthouses, newspapers, and search services with stored public data to make an informed and solid judgment of potential.

Raising major gifts for an institution is an outcome of positive and open relationship management. The sooner the relationship begins, the better.

---

## Potential donor solicitation

Is there a right time to ask for a major gift? Is there a right time to accept one?

For years Mr. Merlot, owner of a large winery in the state, has been a trustee of your institution. In that time he has been moderately philanthropic to your activities in cancer research and hospice, which are high institutional priorities. But you know he has the capacity to make a major gift. You move your strategy forward and, in a joint call with your university president, solicit Merlot for a $1 million endowed cancer research fund. The solicitation call goes as planned. Merlot wants some time to consider his ability and interest in making such a large commitment of personal resources. He insists he will give you an answer in thirty days.

Within a week of your appointment with the prospective donor, a story breaks in the print and TV media of sexual harassment of women at the winery. Activists call a regional boycott and the story continues for several days. The accusations seem to be true.

Although Merlot is not accused personally, his legal and public relations advisers counsel him to do something to cast a positive light on the winery. As a result, he decides to act on your request for a million-dollar gift. However, he offers to make a $2 million corporate gift to endow a faculty professorship in the maternal and child health program rather than in cancer research. The maternal and child health program is an equally high priority of your institution.

Corporate philanthropy has often been labeled enlightened self-interest. Both programs—cancer research and maternal and child health—are institutional priorities. Merlot's winery needs some positive publicity. Are both institutions' interests satisfied by a major gift?

Charitable intent and institutional betterment are the points of analysis to determine whether this gift transaction is an ethical transaction. The code of behavior followed in creating a potential donor discovery and research program must also apply to gift solicitation and acceptance practice.

Merlot is in legal trouble and is looking for a partner to help minimize the damage to his personal and corporate reputation. Can you help him? Ethically, I think you can.

As development officer, your job is to secure philanthropic gifts. Key major gift fundraising activities are asking for (the easy part) and closing (the hard part) major gifts and placing into service the funds or property received in response to a request. Often, between these two separate fundraising actions, time exists for negotiation. Negotiations on gift timing and payment terms, the language of the gift or endowment agreement, gift size, etc., are part of the solicitation-to-gift-closure process. These negotiations can work to minimize Merlot's public relations dilemma. Donor and charity gift discussions that are sensitive to timing may even result in an increase to the original gift request.

After careful research and preparation, Merlot was asked for a major gift for a high institutional priority. In closing the gift, Merlot should be asked to revisit your original solicitation meeting and to review and respond to the proposal you made: an endowed cancer research program. A $2 million gift will better your institution and, perhaps, support the development of new therapies or cures for cancer affecting the health of women. Merlot, although not motivated solely by charitable intent, might still have had such charitable intent if the winery's personnel problems had not surfaced when they did.

In accepting a modified gift of $2 million for cancer research affecting the health of women, have you achieved "enlightened self-interest" for both Merlot and the institution? Can you hold your institutional head up ethically?

## Gift stewardship

Institutional leaders have a responsibility to their donors to carry out the relevant program, research, care, or educational activity in return for their philanthropic support. Gift stewardship is the method of fulfilling this moral contract.

Conservatively, stewardship incorporates gift acknowledgment and recognition, and gift management. I attempt to identify the ethical questions we might consider with each one.

For me, the most troubling of the two is gift acknowledgment and recognition. Many universities and other not-for-profits set rules for the level of gift required to be recognized with a named endowment or named building, room, etc. Unfortunately, those rules are often broken in hot pursuit of a charitable gift. Fundraisers use naming opportunities in presenting proposals and in negotiating gifts at the time of gift closure.

The main goal in securing transforming gifts—those that endow programs of great stature and build great facilities of research promise—is the maintenance of institutional integrity. Our governing boards and our professional colleagues must develop consistent and practiced institutional gift policies. Policies can be changed with thoughtful review. If we accommodate a change in gift policy to recognize one donor, we harm those donors already in the fold, now and in the future. Word gets out quickly that an institution has "sold" a naming opportunity for a bargain price. Institutional reputations are made on integrity, and they can be lost through philanthropic indiscretion.

How do we make sure our professional and institutional integrity remains intact? Here are some guidelines:

- Be clear about your mission and goals.
- Share your philanthropic objectives.
- Develop a complete gift policy manual for donors, volunteers, and staff that identifies acceptable gifts and the method for acknowledgment and recognition.

- If desired by the donor, publicly recognize gifts with naming opportunities. State how those gifts met your institutional gift policy.
- Thank all donors regardless of gift size.

## Gift management

Gifts are becoming much more restricted than they were a decade or two ago. Donors find it intriguing and emotionally stimulating to support specific areas of research or education in an institution; unrestricted gifts are stagnating. Donors to Duke Medical Center, for example, are now restricting their gifts more than 90 percent of the time—to cancer research, cardiac care, etc. This modern phenomenon requires sophisticated systems for tracking and reporting the use of these gift funds. Thankfully, excellent gift recording and receipting systems have been developed and information management and distribution systems make this stewardship responsibility easier.

However, there are potential major ethical hurdles to consider. First, restricted gifts: If we cannot use gifts, is it ethical to retain them—or accept them in the first place? Second, conservative endowment investment policies: Are we planning for the rainy day and missing opportunities to invest in new things today?

## Relationships between donors and development officers

A critical ethical dilemma may emerge as a relationship between the donor and the development officer matures. A donor may express friendship through an offer of gratuities: travel on a private plane, a weekend at a summer cottage, etc. These gratuities, perhaps meaningless to the donor, might compromise the development officer's ability to carry out his or her responsibilities to secure philanthropy for a charitable organization. The development officer has a great amount of freedom to observe the behaviors and tendencies of an organization's best friends: the donors helping advance a project or program of importance to the charity. Is a gratuity a siphoning away of potential support to the organization? Should the development officer turn a gratuity into a new gift for the organization? If accepted, how should it be reported within an organization? If acceptable, how should the development officer share the gratuity among colleagues, including support staff?

Answering ethical questions like these is best accomplished through a study of the organizational philosophy and code of behavior of the charity. Accepting a donor's gratuity is an ethical dilemma for the development officer if organizational policy forbids such activity. The relationship between the development officer and the donor matures through mutual interest in a charity of the donor's choosing. The donor makes gifts to the charity and the development officer secures gifts as the charity's public emissary. In making an ethical judgment, consider this question: Would the same relationship exist without the charity? If yes, a gift is a donor's demonstration of friendship. If no, the gratuity must be politely refused.

## Conclusion

Major gift development is much more complex than asking for an annual commitment to your cause or program. The ethical dilemmas are also complex. Our institutions, many of which have been founded by philanthropic commitments, are seeking increasingly large sums of support. The billion-dollar comprehensive campaign is becoming more common among major research universities, public and private. As the pressure builds to produce these incredible sums, the development profession must be a bedrock of ethical practice. "Is it right and moral?" should be the thought we wake up to and fall asleep with.

JOSEPH S. BEYEL *is vice chancellor of Duke University Medical Center for development and alumni affairs.*

*An overview of women's motivations and potential as major philanthropic donors, including specific recommendations for involving more women as major donors.*

# 5

# Women as philanthropists: Leading the transformation in major gift fundraising

*Martha A. Taylor, Sondra C. Shaw*

OVER THE AGES, women have been giving of their time and money to better society. For example, thirteenth-century religious women of wealth founded hospitals and homes to assist the poor in cities across Europe (Moerschbaecher, 1996). In the United States, Emma Willard endowed Troy Female Seminary in 1821, the first endowed girls' school in the country to offer mathematics, history, and languages. Mary Lyon founded Mount Holyoke Seminary in 1837. Jane Addams created Hull House in 1889 to aid immigrants and other disadvantaged individuals as they settled into the rough city of Chicago. With one strategically planned gift, Mary Elizabeth Garrett raised the standards for practicing medicine and opened the field to women. When the Johns Hopkins University needed $500,000 to open a medical school in the late nineteenth century, Garrett donated $350,000 on the condition that the institution require a bachelor's degree for admissions and enroll women

NEW DIRECTIONS FOR PHILANTHROPIC FUNDRAISING, NO. 16, SUMMER 1997 © JOSSEY-BASS PUBLISHERS

with the same rigorous standards for admission and matriculation as men (Fisher, 1993).

The tradition of women's major gift philanthropy continues today with the efforts of such individuals as Maddie Levitt and Oseola McCarty. Levitt launched the $131 million Campaign for Drake University with a major challenge gift for the trustees. They responded by exceeding the challenge in a few short weeks. Levitt was the first woman to chair a campaign of such magnitude for a coeducational institution. She was recognized by the National Society of Fund Raising Executives with the 1995 Outstanding Philanthropist Award.

A laundress for most of her eighty-seven years, Oseola McCarty earned her living a few dollars at a time (Bragg, 1995). As a child she had to quit school in the sixth grade to support her family. In 1995, she was honored in the White House by President Clinton for her donation of $150,000 to the University of Southern Mississippi to fund scholarships for African American students. She wanted to help today's young people complete their education; inspired by her generosity, local businesses have matched her gift, doubling its impact.

Despite the contributions of these and countless other women, women's philanthropy was largely invisible until a few years ago. No monetary value was placed on women's extensive volunteer service in churches, schools, hospitals, and soup kitchens. Because in the past few women had ownership of their fortunes or the legal right to make financial decisions on their own, many philanthropic gifts of money were credited in history to their husbands.

What has changed in recent years is that more women now have control over their money through inheritance. As women increasingly move into the corporate and professional worlds, they begin to recognize their tremendous potential to apply charitable dollars to shape the future of society. A tradition of caring coupled with financial control is altruism with empowerment. The women-and-philanthropy movement is the final frontier of the women's movement.

## Women are givers

In addition to anecdotes about the achievements of individual female philanthropists, there is new statistical evidence about women's giving. The most recent figures released by INDEPENDENT SECTOR show a clear increase in philanthropic donations by women (Gray, 1996). A national survey conducted by the Gallup organization found that women's average annual charitable contribution increased from $781 in 1993 to $983 in 1995, a 26 percent increase. The average gift from men increased by only 6 percent in the same period, from $996 to $1,057. Women now give 93 percent as much annually as men.

Women donated 2.3 percent of their annual income to charity in 1995, while men gave 2.1 percent; it was the first year that women donated a larger share of their income than did men.

In addition to financial commitment, women are still more likely to contribute volunteer time to the causes and institutions they believe in: 52 percent of women versus 45 percent of men volunteered in 1995. The INDEPENDENT SECTOR study also found that those who volunteer were more likely to give financially as well.

Women are indeed taking on an ever-more important role as major donors and prospects for our nonprofit institutions.

## Women have wealth

Women have money. In the United States, 43 percent of people classified by the Internal Revenue Service as top wealth holders are women. The women in this group are 6 percent wealthier than the men, and they are considerably less in debt (Johnson and Schwartz, 1993). Women own one-third of the privately held businesses in the United States and employ 15.5 million people. That's 35 percent more than the Fortune 500 companies employ worldwide, according to a study by the National Foundation for Women Business Owners and Dun & Bradstreet Information Services (National

Foundation for Women Business Owners, 1995, 1996). Women can be expected to come into more wealth as some $10–13 trillion is passed from one generation to the next in the coming twenty-five to fifty years (Avery and Rendall, 1993; Philanthropic Initiative, 1995). Women, who outlive men by an average of seven years, will be making many of the decisions about how this money is dispensed.

Having established that women are givers and have the means to give generously, we confront the question as to why many women hold back in their charitable giving. Why is it that women don't respond to conventional major gift fundraising appeals? Why are those programs that reflect the traditional interests of women—for instance social services, religion, the family—so painfully under-funded?

## Barriers to women's giving

The barriers women face in giving include perceptions women themselves have about their financial situation or their role in society. Many women do not understand financial management—or at least they think they do not understand. Consequently, they are concerned about the possibility of making a decision that could deplete their funds (the "bag lady" syndrome). Many women defer to their husbands, fathers, or financial advisors when making a financial decision. Because parity in giving does not exist in many households, boys' and men's schools are much better endowed than the institutions created to serve women and girls. Other barriers are consumerism and lifestyle choices, which are not necessarily gender specific. However, women exert considerable control over the consumer budget in most families.

Women are not generally socialized to become philanthropists in our society. They see their community role as one of volunteer service (the "bake sale" mentality). The volunteers who plan events and stuff envelopes behind the scenes are not generally considered for the more influential decision-making volunteer roles, including membership on governing boards. It is the responsibility of development officers to help women expand their philanthropic role to include both significant financial giving and volunteer service in a leadership capacity.

To lead this effort, there are good role models in every community. For example, a 1996 focus group study by Andrea Kaminski and Martha Taylor of twenty-five women community volunteer leaders in Madison, Wisconsin, found that 84 percent volunteer five or more hours per week. More than a quarter of these leaders donate twenty or more hours per week to their volunteer causes. They reported an average financial donation of 6.4 percent of their household income to charitable causes, with 20 percent of the group giving 10 percent or more.

To look at a university population, statistics from a ten-year period at the University of Wisconsin-Madison demonstrate a measure of women's giving. A study by Taylor found that women made up half the student body at the university and 40 percent of the alumni in 1991. Yet only 26 percent of those in prospect tracking—those who received a personal visit once a year—were women. Women made up 14 percent of the boards and key committees at the UW Foundation. Nonetheless, 39 percent of the donors during that decade were women, and they donated 36 percent of the total gift dollars.

Imagine the possibilities if more women were personally asked to give, or if more women were represented in the leadership of the institution!

## Why women give

To learn more about women's motivations and giving patterns, the authors conducted extensive interviews and focus groups with women philanthropists and development officers. Women were asked how they had learned about giving, how they make philanthropic decisions, and their attitudes about different fundraising techniques. The findings were compared with those from other coed institutions, including the University of California at Los Angeles (Sublett and Stone, 1992), Cornell University (Menschel, 1992), and the University of Michigan, as well as with those of colleagues at women's funds across the United States and women's colleges, including Wellesley College, which had just completed a $168 million capital campaign (Tanner, 1992).

The women philanthropists communicated a clear message about fundraising: they did not believe their interests were being reflected in the fundraising approach, the campaign goals, or even the projects to be funded. They believed that conventional fundraising techniques have been developed using a male model for the donor. Development officers have been trained to raise money from men. Conventional approaches to fundraising typically appeal to male motivations. A modern, successful female model for philanthropy had yet to emerge.

To develop such a model, development officers must understand women's philanthropic motivations and giving patterns: why they give, what kinds of projects they support, how they prefer to be asked and acknowledged, and what fundraising techniques they abhor. Women's motivations can be summarized in six words beginning with the letter *c*: create, change, connect, collaborate, commit, and celebrate (Shaw and Taylor, 1995).

### Create

Women are philanthropic entrepreneurs. They like to create something with their giving, just as the early women philanthropists created hospitals and educational institutions that continue to live and serve others long beyond the mortal lives of their founders. Some women give to create programs within a larger institution. An example is Lorene Burkhart, who funded a center at Purdue University that studies the effect of legislation and government policy on families.

To appeal to women philanthropists' entrepreneurial instincts, the development officer should inform women donors about new projects and proposals at the institution.

## Change

Women want to use their philanthropic dollars to bring about change. Men are more likely to give out of a sense of loyalty to preserve an institution they care about. Women are somewhat loyal but are more likely to fund a specific program that promises to bring about change, rather than provide unrestricted funds.

Explain to women donors how programs address societal needs and promise change.

## Connect

Women often want a direct connection with the program or project they fund. They want to know how money will be used, how the project is progressing, and how it is helping people. Help your donors feel connected with newsletters, site visits, and individual reports by phone, letter, or in person. An added benefit of these communication techniques is that they provide personal recognition while they help the donor feel connected with the cause.

## Collaborate

Women like to collaborate, or work together as a group. This in part explains why women do not respond to competitive fundraising appeals: they are not interested in topping a peer's gift. Quite the opposite—many women prefer to pool their gifts to make a project possible.

An example is the women lawyers project at the University of Virginia Law School. Some women graduates of this institution believe their presence and tradition in the school has not been adequately acknowledged. For instance, few women are represented in the portraits and plaques in the meeting rooms and corridors. About a year ago, a group of women graduates of the law school collaborated on a project to encourage their women classmates to help fund a highly visible lobby in the school's new building. The fund has exceeded $500,000, and the women's names will be on the wall to commemorate their presence in the school and their collaborative philanthropy (Kingdon, 1995).

### Commit

Women are committed to the causes they support. They want to give not only their money but also their time. This commitment to volunteerism is a result of socialization that values women's service to the community. It goes back to the days when all that women had to contribute was their time. In the authors' focus groups, several women expressed disappointment because they do not believe nonprofits recognize their worth as a volunteer.

Development officers must educate women about the financial needs of the institution and the concept of full philanthropy—giving of both time and money. At the same time, they must validate women's voluntary service. They should listen to women donors, find out how they would like to be involved, and suggest meaningful volunteer opportunities.

### Celebrate

Finally, women like to celebrate their accomplishments and have fun. Again, this goes back to the days when all that women could give was their time, so they raised money with charity balls and bake sales. Major gifts are not raised through events. Women volunteers are now learning how to give and how to ask others for major gifts. Use events to recognize and involve major donors, not to raise money.

Other characteristics of women donors include an expectation of accountability from the organizations they support. Women tend to ask for a lot of specifics. They continue to want detailed information after the gift has been made. Often these women don't really want detailed accountability as much as they want information, which can be provided through newsletters and an occasional phone call.

Women also want personal recognition for their gift. Most prefer to avoid public recognition. It is crucial to send personal thank-you notes and acknowledgments. It is also very important to address these acknowledgments to the woman who made the gift—not to her husband.

Women do not like solicitations based on peer pressure, competition, or public recognition. Fundraisers who rely on these techniques are likely to offend women donors. When trying to reach and motivate women donors, it is important to understand the differences between the way women and men communicate (Tannen, 1991). For example, women tend to engage in "rapport talk" and men in "report talk." In general, women approach a discussion by building rapport with the person to whom they are talking. They often try to identify shared interests and outlook. Men are more likely to report—to provide their own outlook without regard to whether or not the other person shares their view. It is helpful for development officers to understand these differences in communication style before approaching a donor. Philanthropist and educator Tracy Gary says that women take ten times longer than men to make a decision on a major gift, but then bring ten friends to the cause.

Although the issues discussed here came up repeatedly in the focus groups, it would be disastrous to assume that all women donors are alike. Each donor must be approached as an individual. Listen to your donors to learn more about them. Also be aware of demographic trends that often differentiate one generation of women donors from another. A good source of information about the demographics of donors is Judith Nichols's book *Global Demographics* (1995).

## Demographics of women donors

Women born between 1910 and 1930 were profoundly influenced by the Great Depression. They saw fortunes lost overnight and families ruined financially. This experience informs their values and their beliefs about money and sharing. Many of these women worked during the depression and while men were fighting in World War II. But then they spent many years at home raising their children. These women are traditionalist in their views: they may indeed give out of a sense of loyalty. However, they often give to the institutions their husbands were affiliated with, often anonymously or in the husband's name. These women are likely to include men family members or financial advisors in their financial decision making. Acknowledge and affirm these women's values and their contributions of both volunteer time and financial resources. Recognize their gifts with a personal thank-you note and personal attention.

Between 1931 and 1945 the "new older woman," or "builder," was born (Shaw and Taylor, 1991; DMA Non-Profit Council, 1996). This is the woman donor who may have forged a career straight from college in the days before affirmative action, or as a midlife entrant into the professional or business world. She is used to being first: the first woman in her law firm, the first woman vice president in her company, the first woman on the corporate board. She often gives out of loyalty to an institution but prefers to restrict her gift to a program of her choice that promises change. Her philanthropic interests are likely to be women's issues, child welfare, and education. The new older woman may be wary of issues of money and power; she has seen both misused. She appreciates some public recognition—an award at a dinner or her name on a list—but wants personal recognition as well. Never pass up an opportunity to let her know personally how important her contribution is.

The years 1946 to roughly 1964 brought about the baby boom in the United States. This large and powerful segment of the population was influenced by the turbulent 1960s and the Vietnam War. Women—and men—in this group tend to be community oriented. They are committed to bringing about societal change, just as they were twenty-five years ago. The difference is that now the baby boomers are coming into some wealth, and they can apply their excess dollars to the causes they care so much about. Boomer women are more comfortable than older women with money and power, and most boomer women are accustomed to making their own financial decisions. However, boomers absolutely do not give out of a sense of loyalty—this is the generation that questions authority and demands accountability.

When working with baby boomers, show how a project will bring about change. Always listen to and acknowledge their concerns. Never make assumptions: ask them how they wish to be acknowledged.

The "baby busters" were born between 1965 and 1975. Little prospect research has been conducted on this group, and the studies have not been broken down by gender. The baby busters' lifestyle is high tech, and their decision making is very independent. They don't have much money yet, but they are altruistic. Their philanthropic interests include religion and issues related to health and quality of life (Stehle, 1996). They look for quality and stability in nonprofit organizations. They expect to receive a lot of information, preferably over the Internet.

### Reaching women through partnership fundraising

There are two approaches to fundraising: the highly technical approach and the partnership approach. Technically oriented fundraisers focus on the bottom line and think with a sales mind-set. They refer to people as "targets." They are interested in getting the largest dollar amount from a particular gift without concern for developing a long-term relationship between the donor and the institution. These fundraisers don't have time to help empower a female donor.

Then there are fundraisers who believe in building partnerships. They know that in a world with so many needs and so many good causes to give to, the institution that respects the donor as an individual—not as a target—stands out. The donor can tell this is the kind of institution that can actually help her give her money away, knowing it will make a difference. This is the approach women donors prefer.

The secret of the women's philanthropy movement is that many men don't like the technical approach to fundraising either. The giving attitudes and patterns of baby boomer men and younger men are more similar to those of women than to those of their fathers (Nichols, 1995). These men don't like competition or peer pressure any more than women do, although as men they have been socialized to respond to these techniques.

Women have been socialized to respond to the needs they see around them. Through their philanthropic giving, women will lead a transformation of the fundraising profession. To motivate this new breed of donor, nonprofits have to rise above appeals to the ego or names on buildings to show how their programs address societal needs. Development officers have to be technically competent, but they must take the time to build strong philanthropic partnerships with their major donors. Development officers have to return to the core values that inspired them to enter the profession—notably the desire to make the world a better place. This is what women donors demand.

## Summary

In conclusion, women differ from men in giving in that they are more concerned with the cause than the legacy or recognition for their philanthropic act. More men create foundations in their own names and give ultimate gifts for named buildings or activities.

Women are powerful volunteers who open doors of opportunity for institutions and ask other individuals for major gifts. Good listening skills and sensitivity to female communication methods are essential when working with women donors. Solicitation for gifts from women should differ depending upon the woman's age, level and source of wealth, life stage, and career status.

Are women more altruistic than men? Women have long been socialized to be the nurturers and caretakers of people in our society. When this altruism meets financial empowerment, women will reach their fullest potential as philanthropists, and a better society for future generations will be the result.

## References

Avery, R. B., and Rendall, M. S. "Estimating the Size and Distribution of Baby Boomers' Prospective Inheritances." *Proceedings of the Annual Meeting of the American Statistical Association,* 1993, pp. 11–19.

Bragg, R. "All She Has, $150,000, Is Going to a University." *New York Times,* Aug. 13, 1995, pp. 1, 11.

DMA Non-Profit Council. *The Heart of the Donor: A Lifestage Analysis.* New York: Russ Reid Co., Barna Research Group, January 1996.

Fisher, J. M. "Celebrating the Heroines of Philanthropy." In A. I. Thompson and A. R. Kaminski (eds.), *Women and Philanthropy: A National Agenda.* Madison: Center for Women and Philanthropy, University of Wisconsin, 1993.

Gray, S. "Charities See Bigger Gifts, Fewer Givers." *Chronicle of Philanthropy,* Oct. 17, 1996, pp. 9–12.

Johnson, B. W., and Schwartz, M. "Personal Wealth, 1989." *Statistics of Income (SOI) Bulletin.* Washington, D.C.: U.S. Internal Revenue Service, 1993, p. 105.

Kingdon, M. "Women Lawyers Pool Gifts." *Women's Philanthropy* (newsletter of National Network on Women as Philanthropists), Dec. 1995, pp. 5–6.

Menschel, R. *Women as Contributors to Higher Education.* Report. Ithaca, N.Y.: Cornell University, 1992.

Moerschbaecher, L. S. "Don't You Worry Your Pretty Little Head." Presentation. LMNOP Seminars and Publications, San Rafael, Calif., 1996.

National Foundation for Women Business Owners. Press releases. Washington, D.C.: National Foundation for Women Business Owners, 1995, 1996.

Nichols, J. E. *Global Demographics: Fund Raising for a New World.* Chicago: Bonus Books, 1995.

Philanthropic Initiative. *The Ten Trillion Dollar Intergenerational Transfer of Wealth: A Philanthropic Game Plan.* Boston: Philanthropic Initiative, 1995.

Shaw, S. C., and Taylor, M. A. "Career Women: A Changing Environment for Philanthropy." *NSFRE Journal* (National Society of Fund Raising Executives), Fall 1991, pp. 43–49.

Shaw, S. C., and Taylor, M. A. *Reinventing Fundraising: Realizing the Potential of Women's Philanthropy.* San Francisco: Jossey-Bass, 1995, pp. 83–100.

Stehle, V. "'Baby Busters' Demand More from Charities, Study Finds." *Chronicle of Philanthropy,* Feb. 8, 1996, p. 25.

Sublett, D., and Stone, K. *The UCLA Women and Philanthropy Focus Groups.* Report. Los Angeles: University of California at Los Angeles, 1992.

Tannen, D. *You Just Don't Understand: Women and Men in Conversation.* New York: Ballantine, 1991.

Tanner, N. "Are Wellesley Women Different?" *Wellesley Alumnae Newsletter,* 1992.

MARTHA A. TAYLOR *is vice president of the University of Wisconsin Foundation.*

SONDRA C. SHAW, *adjunct professor of public affairs at Western Michigan University, recently retired as that university's assistant vice president of external affairs. With Taylor, she is coauthor of* Reinventing Fundraising: Realizing the Potential of Women's Philanthropy *and (also with Taylor) a founding board member of the Women's Philanthropy Institute, which brings together philanthropists and fundraisers to educate, encourage, and empower women to express their values through their financial giving and volunteer leadership.*

*The greatest challenge facing America's philanthropic community today is to attract CEOs and trustees who have both the capacity and the commitment to lead the institution and then to provide and attract truly significant support.*

# 6

# CEOs and trustees: The key forces in securing major gifts

*G. T. "Buck" Smith*

EVERY ORGANIZATION HAS TWO fundamental needs: a meaningful and clearly articulated *vision* and appropriate *resources* to fulfill it. It is the responsibility of enlightened leadership—from the CEO and board of trustees—to assure that both are in place.

Sadly enough, too many not-for-profits plunge right in with trying to draft a mission statement. But before the mission there must first be a vision—a clear sense of what higher purposes might be served, of how lives might be changed, of how the broader human condition might be enhanced.

These are illusive issues, often difficult to get our minds and words around. But it is these visionary possibilities that ultimately stir the hearts and lift the imaginations of those who will provide necessary resources. Clarity and articulation are requisite for the CEO and trustees to achieve success in securing major gifts.

NEW DIRECTIONS FOR PHILANTHROPIC FUNDRAISING, NO. 16, SUMMER 1997 © JOSSEY-BASS PUBLISHERS

## The chief executive officer

An organization's success depends in large measure on the chief executive's enthusiasm and capacity for leadership in helping secure major gift support. In this role, the CEO must provide both initiative and inspiration, focusing primarily on three essential tasks:

1. Articulating clearly and convincingly the organization's vision, mission, and goals
2. Enthusiastically nurturing relationships with potential major gift donors
3. Involving members of the board in helping attract significant gift support

### Vision, mission, and goals

We have noted the importance of clearly setting forth a higher vision toward which individual as well as collective efforts of the organization are directed. As the primary planner, the chief executive needs also to take responsibility for developing an appropriate mission statement, clarifying the broad range of institutional priorities, and determining specific areas and projects to receive major support.

In firming up the mission statement, it is important of course to have wide input and counsel from within the organization as well as from representatives of important and appropriate constituencies. Even so, it is the chief executive who must sharpen the focus and make certain the words of the mission statement reflect accurately and concisely (ideally in no more than one brief sentence) what the organization intends for itself. It is especially important that the CEO have this "ownership" in the mission statement inasmuch as he or she is the primary person in articulating it to potential major benefactors.

All too often, the statement of what an organization is about goes on for several paragraphs—sometimes pages. But the attention span of even the most interested persons is limited. Many well-done mission statements require only a single sentence. For example, one university was able to limit its expectations to no more than fifteen words: "To provide liberal and professional learning of distinction within a caring and value-centered community." Even after several years of periodic review by the campus community, these words continued to serve as the central guide to institutional decision making.

Of no less importance is the chief executive's essential role in clarifying the values that shape and guide the institution. It is increasingly acknowledged in the corporate world that the most important role of the chief executive is to manage the values of the organization. Unfortunately, in the nonprofit world, we tend to so democratize the management process that such issues are often consigned to a committee. The outcome ends up partly, if not wholly, inadequate.

Many organizations have their own special cultural dimension reflecting the values and principles of their leaders. For example, one CEO might infuse the organization with a regard only for the highest standards of performance; another, believing fervently that most people most of the time are trying to do the right thing, will have a profound effect on the spirit of that institution. The essential element in setting an organization's values is that the chief executive must care passionately about certain things and then see to it that they are made real.

An institution's mission and values must be not only felt but also continuously stated and restated in public appearances, private conversation, and writing. In this, the short-term chief executive is at a clear disadvantage, because it normally takes years for those in the larger community to fully grasp this deeper dimension of an organization or of its leader. But such awareness is essential if community members are to care deeply about the institution and make serious commitments to it.

### Nurturing major gifts

The chief executive's active involvement is essential in cultivating and soliciting major gift support. There may be those rare situations in which the chief executive can be passive in securing major gifts. But generally, he or she must see this as a primary priority and, owing to the fact that 90 percent or more of total gift results normally are in the form of special and major gifts, make certain that a proportionate share of resources (staff, time, and budget) is allocated accordingly. Unfortunately, very few CEOs have made this level of commitment. For those who have, the results are extraordinary.

To cause such a turnaround requires the force of the chief executive's example. Of primary importance is allocation of the chief executive's time. It is not an overstatement to suggest that few organizations can afford to have less than 60 percent of the chief executive's time devoted to nurturing potential major donors. Those who spend less are likely to do so at their organization's peril; those who spend more will likely prevail.

Too few CEOs of not-for-profit organizations seem to recognize that their success as a leader is often tied directly to their success in raising funds—especially major gifts. It is here that one can most clearly make a noticeable and measurable difference.

There are specific actions a CEO might consider to help achieve success in securing major gifts.

*Take control of the calendar.* The immediate seems always to crowd out the important. Since no task is more important for the CEO than nurturing major gift donors, it must receive priority attention. Too often, unsolicited demands on our time are allowed to overshadow the initiatives we should be taking. An easy solution is simply to block out three days of each week and then allow only nurturing of potential major gift donors to be scheduled on those days. Some CEOs have tried to ease into such a shift in their time priorities, but that seldom works. It is best to do it "cold turkey" and let the rest of the organization adapt.

For years, I blocked out Tuesday through Thursday of each week to do what *I* believed was most important: nurture key relationships. It was remarkable to see that somehow the appointments and meetings that required my presence could almost always be scheduled on Mondays and Fridays. The choice of which three days can vary for each CEO, but a decision *not* to take charge of the calendar is not an option.

*Make personal calls and send handwritten notes.* E-mail is efficient. But it seldom is appropriate in nurturing potential major donors. Even having support personnel place phone calls to those with whom we hope to build a personal relationship is undermining. Donor cultivation is not high tech; it is a highly personal business and requires our *personal* engagement.

Handwritten notes are often far more meaningful to the recipient than typed communications. Mass-generated computer letters are almost always transparent. In contrast, handwritten notes on "hanger" cards (with one's business card printed on the front flap) are especially helpful when enclosing an article or other item of interest to the donor.

*Schedule lunch for four people.* Most people eat lunch each day. But few manage to use that daily occurrence with disciplined intention. Regularly scheduled (at least weekly) lunches with a potential donor or donor couple and a trustee or other key person, in the CEO's office (or adjacent small conference room), can be highly effective, especially when combined with a facilities tour, program rehearsal, etc.

Why lunch for only four people? With any more, one is trying to juggle too many relationships. For example, when one is alone, only one "relationship" exists; when two persons interact, there are two relationships; when three, there are six; when four, there are twelve; when five, twenty; and so on. The ideal maximum would seem to be three persons, because beyond six interactive relationships candor and openness noticeably diminish.

### Meaningful involvement of the board

Inasmuch as a not-for-profit organization rises or falls on the strength of its governing board, the recruitment of trustees is a nonprofit chief executive's most important task. When recruiting board members, we must follow the same principles necessary for staffing any soundly organized enterprise. To ensure that the board has the capacities and strength required, specific expectations should be determined for each trustee position *before* an invitation to membership is extended.

The following criteria have proved useful when recruiting trustees for success in major gifts:

*Financial independence.* Ideally, at least two-thirds of the board membership should be financially independent and capable of significant gift support.

*Time.* All board members should expect, and be expected, to be actively involved in the overall advancement effort. At least one-fourth of the board should be eager, and able, to devote almost unlimited time to helping nurture potential major gift donors.

*Influence.* Every trustee should be part of important and complementing spheres of influence within the institution's primary constituencies. Each trustee should have the stature to ask others for important support.

We must remember that boards of trustees do not give to organizations and institutions; *individual* trustees give to people and ideas and causes in which they believe and about which they care deeply. It is the chief executive's special responsibility always to regard trustees as very special human beings, each with his or her own needs, concerns, hopes, feelings, and aspirations.

To this end, it is essential that we avoid ever taking for granted trustees or their relationships with the institution. To reduce this risk, the chief executive should develop a clear plan for continuously keeping trustees and their spouses informed, sustaining their interest, and involving them in the life of the organization. If done thoughtfully and systematically, investment will surely follow.

By way of illustration, one CEO found it very helpful to carefully assess the board in terms of those who could make what was believed to be the greatest difference for the organization. The board was divided into four groupings, and an intentional plan of personal interaction by the CEO was designed as follows:

| | |
|---|---|
| Top 10 percent | at least weekly |
| Next 20 percent | at least biweekly |
| Next 30 percent | at least monthly |
| Next 40 percent | at least bimonthly |

After four years of carefully nurturing the trustees' relationships with the institution and the CEO, a $54 million campaign was launched (the largest ever for an organization of that size and nature). It concluded at just over $56 million, with $33 million contributed by members of the board, including 16 gifts of $1 million or more.

Later, when the *Chronicle of Higher Education* published a two-page feature on this record of extraordinary trustee giving, most board members who were interviewed attributed their generosity to the deep and meaningful relationship they had with the institution and its CEO.

Clearly, an organization's success does indeed depend on the chief executive officer's enthusiasm and capacity for leadership in helping secure major gift support.

## *Board of trustees*

If the criteria for recruitment of board members have been carefully followed, and their relationships with the institution have been sensitively and consistently nurtured, an organization should be well positioned for trustees to contribute and attract truly significant gift support.

The process begins long before a person is invited to membership on the board. It has its origin when he or she first becomes *aware* of the organization. Over time, one acquires a certain *knowledge* about the organization and its programs and people, and this in turn leads to an *interest* in its values, importance, and achievements. At this point, something begins to happen in the heart as well as the head, and the future trustee begins to *care*. Caring leads naturally to an openness—even a desire—to *participate* in the life of the organization, resulting ultimately in *commitment*.

Commitment is of course to the organization as a corporate entity. But more than that, it is also a highly individual and personal thing, a giving of oneself to a cause in which one believes and from which one draws a sense of fulfillment.

As a *corporate* member of the board, there are certain collective issues and responsibilities to be attended to in concert with other board members that position the organization to attract and justify the confidence of potential major donors:

Appointing, supporting, and assessing the CEO
Endorsing the mission statement
Approving long-range plans
Endorsing various aspects of the program
Ensuring the well-being of staff
Ensuring strong financial management
Ensuring that adequate financial resources are in hand
Preserving institutional autonomy
Interpreting the organization to the community
Interpreting the needs of society to the organization
Serving as a court of appeal
Assessing the board's own performance

Attentiveness to this corporate role of board membership is essential to successful engagement as an individual member of the board. As an individual, each board member must consider the special and sometimes unique ways in which he or she can serve the organization. To be a truly valuable board member, each trustee should have four self-expectations:

1. To provide personal encouragement and support to the CEO and other staff
2. To bring to bear one's own insight and guidance in helping plan the future of the organization
3. To personally encourage understanding and support of the organization from individuals within its several constituencies
4. To provide and help obtain significant operating and capital funds

In fulfilling this final self-expectation, a trustee must come to realize that giving—and encouraging others to give—is not primarily an obligation or even a responsibility of board membership. Rather, it must be viewed as an opportunity and high privilege.

This distinction must be clearly understood by every board member. What we are essentially conveying is that a trustee should expect or be expected to do only that which he or she is comfortable doing. We then must work with each board member to discover what that may be. The answers may include inviting a business or social friend to lunch with the CEO; playing golf; attending an event sponsored by the organization; or possibly merely arranging for an appropriate introduction of the CEO or other staff.

One thing every board member *can* do is mention his or her involvement in and enthusiasm for the organization to at least one person each day. The cumulative effect of this simple act over an extended period is almost beyond measure.

Underlying all these possibilities is the relative importance the organization has in each board member's priorities. Ideally, it should rank right after family, church, and profession. It is, of course, understandable that this may not be so when one first joins a board. But given time, it can and likely will evolve.

### *Conclusion*

One of America's best-known philanthropists, Foster McGaw, sent me a letter he had received some years ago from a complete stranger suggesting that he surely must be among the great benefactors of our time. With the letter he enclosed a brief statement attributed to Henry Van Dyke:

> He that planteth a tree is a servant of God.
> He provideth kindnesses for many generations,
> and faces that he hath not seen shall bless him.

So it is with a man or woman who provides essential endowments and builds necessary buildings. It takes a rather special kind of person to make a generous gift or bequest. Ordinary persons, even when they are rich, can't bring themselves to do it. What do they get for their money? What good can it possibly do them? Such financial backing is furnished by persons with faith and vision— persons who are unselfish enough to plant trees whose shade they themselves will never enjoy.

There are indeed such persons. The great fortune for most not-for-profit CEOs and trustees is that they are privileged to know them and to nurture them in the art and joy of major gifts.

G. T. "BUCK" SMITH *began his professional career at Cornell University. He then returned to his alma mater, the College of Wooster, where he served as vice president for fifteen years. From 1977 to 1988, he was president of Chapman University.*

*The motives of donors of large gifts are both simple and complex. What motivates the wealthy is very much what motivates someone at any point along the economic spectrum, but complexities of ability, spirituality, and association come into play in the making of major gifts.*

# 7

## Major donors, major motives: The people and purposes behind major gifts

### Paul G. Schervish

IN THIS CHAPTER, I explain what motivates the charitable giving of the wealthy, or more succinctly, the major motives of major donors. My research over the past twelve years has enabled me to distill an answer that is both simple and complex. The simple part is that what motivates the wealthy is very much what motivates someone at any point along the economic spectrum. Identify any motive that might inspire concern—from heartfelt empathy to self-promotion, from religious obligation to business networking, from passion to

*Note:* I am grateful to the T. B. Murphy Foundation Charitable Trust and the Lilly Endowment for supporting the research reported here, and to Platon E. Coutsoukis, John J. Havens, and Andrew Herman, who graciously worked with me on various aspects of the research reported here. All the norms and identifying information about the persons interviewed in this chapter have been changed. Where real institutions are mentioned, they represent the type of rather than the particular institution.

prestige, from political philosophy to tax incentives—and some millionaires (as well as some nonmillionaires) will make it the cornerstone of their giving. The complex part about the charitable motivation of the wealthy is that those who hold great wealth and consciously direct it to social purposes invariably want to shape rather than merely support a charitable cause. Although everyone who makes a gift wants it to make a difference, those who make a big gift want it to make a big difference. This raises the question, then, about what distinctive additional or complementary mobilizing factors come into play when major donors make major gifts.

Our research on giving and volunteering over the past decade has enabled my colleagues and me to develop several interconnected sets of findings and to specify their practical implications for generating charitable giving. In this chapter, I elaborate on three sets of research findings that are directly related to charting the motivational matrix of the wealthy.

The first set helps us specify an additional motivational vector that is peculiar to those who are able to allocate substantial resources to charity. The distinguishing characteristic of wealth holders is that they are "hyperagents." By this I mean that in addition to being agents alongside the rest of us, living within a given institutional framework, in many realms—from business to politics to philanthropy—they are capable of establishing the institutional framework within which they and others live.

The second set of findings concern what we call the *identification model of caritas*. We have found that the spiritual foundations for charitable giving revolve around identification with the needs of others. Drawing on the writings of Thomas Aquinas and other thinkers, and on an analysis of intensive interviews with millionaires, we perceive that the key to the practice of care is how people link their destiny to the destiny of others. The practice of care derives from the disposition that meeting the needs of others fulfills one's own needs *and* connects one to the deeper dimensions of life, often experienced and expressed in religious terms as the unity of love of self, love of neighbor, and love of God.

Our third set of findings concerns the *associational dynamics of charity*. Our empirical research demonstrates that the forces of identification are generated, nurtured, and manifested through the associational relations of individuals. Generosity of time and money derives not from one's level of income or wealth but from the physical and moral density of one's associational life and horizons of identification.

In this chapter, I draw on the research findings that my colleagues and I have uncovered regarding motivations for charitable giving. My intention is to chart the unique juncture where general charitable motivations intersect with the motivations that are particular to the distinctive financial capacities and social-psychological dispositions of the wealthy. In the first section, I discuss the empowering class trait of the wealthy, which I call hyperagency. In the second section, I illustrate the mobilizing factors that we have found to be at the heart of the identification and association models of charitable giving. Although these factors apply in a general way to donors at all levels of income and wealth, I draw on my intensive interviews with the wealthy to portray how the factors apply specifically to holders of wealth. In the third section I address two topics. First, I describe how the class trait of hyperagency leads wealth holders to an *inclination* to be producers rather than simply supporters of philanthropic projects. Second, I explore how the growing levels of wealth and the estate tax code, as modified by the 1986 Federal Tax Code revisions, combine to become an unprecedented ally of philanthropy. With charitable contributions having become the principal alternative to paying an effective estate tax rate of 60 percent, no discussion of the determinants of major gifts can omit the operation of estate taxes in generating charitable giving. In the conclusion, I indicate some practical implications for encouraging wealth holders to become major donors.

I base the analysis largely on the findings from the Study on Wealth and Philanthropy. This multiyear research project, funded by the T. B. Murphy Foundation, focused on the meaning and practice of money management among individuals with a net worth of

$1 million or more who have earned or inherited their wealth. During the course of the research, we conducted 130 intensive interviews with individuals spread over eleven metropolitan areas of the United States. (See Schervish and Herman, 1988, for details on the sample and methodology of the Study on Wealth and Philanthropy.)

## Major donors: Determination and dominion

"Just who, exactly, did the Dutch think they were?" asks Simon Schama (1988, p. 51) as he begins his exploration of the cultural setting and moral identity of the sixteenth-century and seventeenth-century Dutch who, for the first time in history, composed a whole class of people who were wealthy without being aristocratic. There is in that question, of course, a bit of the acerbic overtone we find in the parental admonition, "Just who do you think you are?" But Schama's question is also an opening for a serious answer. In that spirit, I explore the question "Just who, exactly, do the wealthy think they are?" My answer requires a look at the attributes of determination and dominion that characterize the empowerment of wealth holders.

### Hyperagency

In a famous statement, Karl Marx argued that although people do indeed make their own history, they are not able to choose the conditions under which they do so. Although Marx was referring to collective action, the same dictum holds for individual actors as well. However, the capacity to "make history" is not equally distributed. Some, including wealth holders, make more history than others. I call this history-making capacity of individuals *hyperagency*. For sure, not every hyperagent is wealthy. Some financially common folk make history by virtue of being profound, creative, or spiritual. But in the material realm, every wealth holder is at least potentially a hyperagent.

Hyperagency refers to the enhanced capacity of wealthy individuals to establish or control substantially the conditions under which they and others live. For most individuals, agency is limited to choosing among and acting within the constraints of those situations in which they find themselves. As monarchs of agency, the wealthy can circumscribe such constraints and, for good or ill, create for themselves a world of their own design. As everyday agents, most of us strive to *find* the best possible place to live or the best job to hold, within a given field of possibilities. As hyperagents, the wealthy—when they choose to do so—can *found* a broad array of the field of possibilities within which they will live and work.

Whenever a respondent is asked to identify the most important attribute of wealth, the answer is invariably the same: *freedom.* Such freedom is both a negative release *from* constraint and a positive capacity *to* secure desire. Negative freedom refers to the loosening or negation of constraints, especially from the immediate pressures surrounding stable provision of material well-being. At the extreme, it is liberty from having to work in order to survive. In contrast, positive freedom refers to the capacity to accomplish desires in the face of constraints. In the material realm, such freedom is the ability to experience virtually every situation, from housing and vacations to education and work, as opportunities for choice rather than conditions of compromise or deprivation. For instance, the fact that the wealthy do not *have* to work ironically results often enough in their *wanting* to work. Freed *from* the obligation to work, they are free *to* select and shape their work so that it becomes a source of satisfaction, self-actualization, and effective accomplishment. Attorney Rebecca Austin (a pseudonym, as are all the vignette names and identifying details in this chapter) expresses this duality of freedom in her assessment of how wealth "smoothes out" the everyday toils of life and enables her to set her "own agenda":

Everything is easier when you have money. It's a shame because it's such a hard thing to get. It is the one item that smoothes out what everyone is struggling for: security, good health, fitness, good relationships, taking care of your children. Work choices are easier. Life is easier. You can do anything you want. You can take a vacation whenever and wherever you want. And even though I have a job, it's the kind of job that I can get there when I want to get there, because I want to be there rather than having to be there. The reason I work at [a public interest firm with the pseudonym] Citizen Law is that I can integrate my life. It allows me to focus on issues and do things that can become all-encompassing in terms of things that I care about. I don't work on anything I don't care about. I don't take assignments from anybody else. I set my own agenda.

To set one's own agenda, especially in those areas where it is usually set by others, is the fundamental endowment of wealth. Wealth enables individuals to freely conceive of and choose from among a wheel of alternatives. It would, of course, be foolish to assert that the possession of wealth dissolves all the fetters of time, health, and social constraint. The wealthy do indeed face constraints and rightly feel bounded in certain ways by obligation and responsibility (see Schervish, 1994). They have concerns with continued and expanded accumulation of wealth, organizational pressures of business, strategies of investment, generational reproduction of family wealth, preservation of a congenial political and economic climate, and moral and social responsibilities of philanthropy. Such concerns do indeed demand their time, money, and consciousness. As Norman Stryker, the Houston-born heir to an oil fortune, says, being granted an inheritance is a surprisingly alien burden. Without quotidian necessity to shape his life, he is forced to "carve out every goddamn day." Still, we find that even those who first flounder about with an inheritance overcome the obstacles and eventually learn the advantages of carving out rather than receiving their daily round.

### Determination: The individuality of psychological empowerment

Although the success of wealthy individuals in making the world requires material riches, it is also contingent upon a constellation of emotional, intellectual, and moral dispositions that enable the rich to act with determination. To be world builders in the spheres of business, consumption, and philanthropy, wealth holders need to learn repertoires of knowledge and sentiment. Del Garrison, a prominent Hollywood actor, describes the impact of wealth upon his consciousness and behavior as having "opened up a world to me that I never knew existed, a world that is not just one of consumption but of understanding! Of seeing the world in a different way. It's an education." The transformation provoked by wealth, he clarifies, "is not so much a value thing as it is a very basic thing" in that he became introduced to a way of life he "either didn't know existed or knew existed but [I thought was only] for somebody else." In the area of food, for instance, his wealth opened up not just new tastes, "some of which I liked and some I didn't," but a whole new cultural horizon. It was "a real mind expander":

As a result of exploring [various foods] I found out about them, where they come from, a little about the cultures they're derived from, and so forth. So that what I meant in a sense is that everything like that, whether it be food or an understanding of the further distance between where I was now and where I had been, I was beginning to be more aware of what I had been and of others who lived that way and would never be out of living that way. It was a real mind expander and I can understand, I think, why often times poverty is such a narrowing thing. Now, I'm not saying I was in poverty, as I never considered myself in poverty, but how poverty can be such a crushing and narrowing thing because it limits all kinds of opportunities so much. I did have a wonderful thing.

Garrison goes on to exemplify this "wonderful thing" by describing an especially satisfying episode in which he kept his underlying empowerment of wealth hidden in reserve until the proper dramatic moment.

I had on an old pair of ratty jeans and a work shirt and some beat up boots. And I was driving down the street and I saw this 4-wheel drive Toyota Land Cruiser in the window of a place and I said "that's what I want, that's what I need." And I walked up in my semi-hippiness and asked the salesman how much it was and he kind of looked at me like, "It's out of your reach, fella." And I kept walking around looking at it, and I said, "Well, how much is it and if I bought it how soon could I get it?" He said, "If you pay cash for it, I'll have it ready for you in an hour." And I said, "OK, I want it." He said, "What?" And I pulled the cash out of my pocket and paid for it. At that time it was a real bubble to be able to do something like that. I haven't done anything like that since. I had to sort of do it once.

Individuality is psychological empowerment. It revolves around the premise of great expectations, the right to pursue them, and conviction about one's ability to achieve them. Individuality is not only a matter of conception; it is a matter of perception: of oneself as a minor demigod who has, at least in some local sphere, burst the bonds of normal agency in constructing the environment. Shaping the world is always in reference to how it shapes or expresses one's self. As Benjamin Ellman, the owner of a hotel supply company in Chicago, says, "I've never thought of doing things because it's the particularly right thing to do—except if it was the right thing for me to do. I've always been a doer. I've always been a leader."

In a world where most individuals are limited to carving out the best possible niche in an organizational scheme designed by others, the wealthy are able to conceive and create a world tailored to their specification. Detroit importer Rebecca Jacobs captures this close affiliation between uninhibited imagination and determined purpose: "I'm a winner, and I believe in winning in life. And I set my own goals. And I'm a dreamer—I think that's one of the big assets that I have, my imagination. It's the most wonderful thing in the world that I have—and I just try to make those dreams come true. I just know I'm going to win. I've been a winner and a dreamer since I was a little girl, and I knew that. You are what you think about. You are what you believe."

A key element of this individuality is a posture of emotional distance from the trials and tribulations of certain daily affairs. The distance from the mundane, explains Detroit heir Hillary Blake, may be so alluring as to be like "magic":

I feel like a little girl and I feel like this is just pie in the sky. You know, this is like Fantasy Land or something like that. It's magic. And I think I should be responsible about it, but I don't want to be. You know what analogy comes to mind? This is going to sound crazy, but it's always fascinated me how radios work because if you're driving in your car and you just turn the knob, a different song comes from nowhere. I'm sure that somebody could explain to me how that happens. But I don't want them to because I like the image that it's—that it's just magic. And that's exactly how I feel when it comes to this part of the money: I know intellectually where all the dividends come from and approximately what they are. And I know what my annual income is, and I know what my expenses are, and I know how much money I give away, and I know how much I pay in taxes, and I know it all. And then all of this stuff gets split off and I live in this fantasy world. I had a girlfriend say to me one time, "You know, there's nothing that you'll be able to do in your life that will earn you more money than staying at home in bed and eating bon-bons." Now I thought, "Well, you know, that's true."

But despite the magical lures of opulence, such emotional liberty seldom if ever leads to the confection-filled complacency she fantasizes. Far from sitting home eating bon-bons, Blake established and helps run the Forest Grove women's foundation in the Detroit area. Emotional liberty, it turns out, actually expedites involvement. For activist attorney Allison Randall, what is "wonderful" about freedom from "financial restrictions" is that it enables her to think expansively about her "next career": "My next career could be anything. I have that freedom and I'm not afraid to sort of think, well, maybe you could do *that*."

"That's the nature of privilege," notes Bradley Stark, thirty-two-year-old heir of a distinguished American family. As though he were answering Randall, Stark advocates a *responsibility* to do things that are as defining as having the potential to do them: "If it's privilege, it's not something [you can abandon]. I mean, obviously you can get rid of money. You can give all your money away and then you're not privileged anymore. But you were privileged to be in that position. So that your giving it away is in itself an exercise of that privilege. So there's really no way of getting around it."

As we have seen with Garrison's purchase of the Land Cruiser, cognitive empowerment provides the orientation that the world is subject to amendment. This is eloquently underscored by attorney Austin, who recognizes that not "dealing with day-to-day" life makes her "a different kind of person"—one more able to deal deliberately with "substantive issues":

The difference for the wealthy is that they are so far removed from the [mundane kinds of] struggle to do what they are doing that it becomes a qualitatively different way of life. And the reason that I know that is that I can see the changes even at my home. We have a housekeeper. One of the things that she does is clean. Every day. I used to clean myself, a lot of years ago. But now I am so used to having it done for me that I take it for granted. [I have reached] that level of beginning to have such a different lifestyle that you have no idea of what people are dealing with day to day. It sure makes a big difference when you get to the top. And when you have generation after generation that has no contact with those kinds of things, it has to make you a different kind of person. I don't know what all of that is like except by watching myself and the kind of freedom that I have to deal with substantive issues.

### Dominion: The principality of temporal and spatial empowerment

The worldly domain in and through which the wealthy "deal with substantive issues" is their *principality*. If individuality revolves around psychological empowerment, principality revolves around temporal and spatial empowerment. If individuality is self-construction, principality is world building.

Temporal empowerment is the longitudinal dimension of principality. It is the ability to influence significant stretches of the past and future, and to make concrete arrangements to extend one's control over the present. This is clear to Detroit wholesaler Brendan Dwyer, who explains that one key to his success is that " I allocate my time. I allocate my time," he repeats, "where I think it will make a difference." Following the adage that "20 percent of the events account for 80 percent of the results," he purposefully tries to "shy away from allocating time to the 80 percent that are only going to account for 20 percent of the results." In this way he can "influence results" *and* retain "a certain amount of time for leisure."

Another expression of temporal empowerment is the familiar penchant of the wealthy to perpetuate their family legacy by arranging for intergenerational transfer of wealth through trusts and other intrafamily mechanisms of inheritance. As Eileen Case Wilson notes, her family wealth, derived from the past, is legally arranged in the present to sustain her lineage into the future:

No non-Case may own stock [in my grandfather's company]. So I cannot pass my stock to my husband, for instance; only to a blood Case, not to their spouses. My mother, for instance, has no stock. She's not a relative. That was grandfather's intent: to safeguard and preserve the family 's corporation. He couldn't control their lives, but he could control who owns Case Chapter, so he only gave stock to his own issue. It still is a condition today. My grandparents left their shares of the business to the five grandchildren in trust, the income of which was to go to my father for the duration of his life. Upon my father's death, those trusts are dissolved and they will come directly to my sister and me—not including what will pass from my father to my children. That income will come to me for the duration of my life, even though the children will own his stock.

Austin and her husband introduce their son to the prospects of temporal empowerment as they counsel him about how his forthcoming inheritance will allow him to freely choose his career. They tell him about "the kind of money he can expect to have" so that he can begin "thinking about career choices and what he wants to do." Because her husband "has worked very hard," says Austin, he "likes the idea of my son being able to choose what he wants to do and not what he feels he has to do. So we have let him know that as he's making his decision, he should be thinking about what it is that he wants to do."

But in addition to extending family and opportunity over time, temporal empowerment provides the capacity to shape the future. According to New York interior decorator Carol Layton, this means perpetuating herself through her business. "I have a need for ongoing things," she explains. "I want the business to go on. I want to build something that doesn't die when I die. So we're building something that we hope will have continuity." Scanning the temporal horizon, the wealthy articulate a range of possible trajectories for practices in different spheres of activity. They project possible futures not only for themselves and their families, but for the businesses and organizations to which they are tied.

*Spatial empowerment* is the geographical counterpart of temporal empowerment. It marks the territorial boundaries of principality. Spatial empowerment refers to both the vertical power exercised within a sphere and horizontal power exercised across spheres of institutional life. In the exercise of spatial power, the wealthy direct and coordinate the monetary and human resources of organizations, strategically mobilizing the use of these resources as material extensions of their will and physical incarnations of their presence. "The [hotel supply] company was built around me," reports Chicagoan Benjamin Ellman. "Everybody in the United States thinks about this company as me personally. I once felt that was wrong, and that there's no way you can be successful in business if things revolve around one individual and you want to grow larger. That's not necessarily true. Look what's happening today. What's happening today with Lee Iacocca and other people. Individuals who are heading up businesses are becoming more connected with their businesses."

"The most important thing money gives me is power to get through time and red-tape barriers," explains real estate magnate Graham Reynolds. Connecting spatial to temporal empowerment, he explains how his wealth reduces the time and distance for getting things done: "I can pick up the phone and call a congressman who's heard my name, and I can have the impact of one million votes on the issue with a phone call. You always have the upper hand in negotiating, and it allows you to do in one-tenth the time what it would take somebody else ten times the time because of the credibility he'd have to develop."

The same is true for another real estate developer, David Stephanov, who also "picks up the phone" to set his will in motion. Exemplifying his Golden Rule—"them with the gold makes the rules"—Stephanov describes how, in addition to injecting himself into the world, spatial empowerment enables him to bring the world to himself. "When I want something, [politicians] come here and meet me for breakfast, and I tell them what I want. When I have to convey a message to the governor, he comes here, or he'll have one of his top two or three aides come down, and I'll tell them what I think should be done. And then we go from there." Whether running a business, exercising executive power in a corporation, or disbursing the funds through a family foundation, the wealthy command actors and resources as they carve out a custom-made dominion.

## Major motives: Identification and association

I have summarized in several publications what my colleagues and I have found to be the major mobilizing factors that generate charitable giving (Schervish 1995, Schervish 1997). Taken together, these mobilizing factors compose what I call the identification model of charitable giving. We have published our first empirical test of the theory (Schervish and Havens, 1997) based on an analysis of the 1991 Survey of Giving and Volunteering (Hodgkinson and Weitzman, 1992). Our findings are that the level of contributions depends on the frequency and intensity of participation, volunteering, and being asked to contribute. Our findings also indicate that larger gifts are generated from those already making substantial gifts. Taken together, our general conclusion is that charitable giving derives from forging an associational and psychological connection between donors and recipients (Ostrander and Schervish, 1990).

I illustrate the identification theory by returning to the data from which I originally generated the theory. This first effort to ascertain the determinants of charitable giving that constitute the identification model was an analysis of intensive interviews with 130 millionaires in the Study on Wealth and Philanthropy. During the course of these interviews, we obtained information both about the modes of empowerment discussed in the previous section and about the factors that motivate giving among millionaires. What we learned provided the basis for inductively mapping a constellation of seven variable-sets that were positively related to charitable giving. These eight sets of variables are listed and briefly described in Exhibit 7.1. Here I illustrate in detail only four of these variable sets, and even then I tend to concentrate on one specific aspect of each set. In this section, I discuss frameworks of consciousness, especially under the cardinal rubric *identification*, and communities

**Exhibit 7.1. Determinants of charitable giving**

1. *Communities of participation*: groups and organizations in which one participates
2. *Frameworks of consciousness*: beliefs, goals, and orientations that shape the values and priorities that determine people's activities
3. *Invitations to participate*: requests by persons or organizations to directly participate in philanthropy
4. *Discretionary resources*: the quantitative and psychological wherewithal of time and money that can be mobilized for philanthropic purposes
5. *Models and experiences from one's youth:* the people or experiences from one's youth that serve as positive exemplars for one's adult engagements
6. *Urgency and effectiveness*: a desire to make a difference; a sense of how necessary or useful charitable assistance will be in the face of people's needs
7. *Demographic characteristics*: the geographic, organizational, and individual circumstances of one's self, family, and community that affect one's philanthropic commitment
8. *Intrinsic and extrinsic rewards*: the array of positive experiences and outcomes (including taxation) of one's current engagement that draws one deeper into a philanthropic identity

*Note:* See Schervish and Havens (in press) for a fuller description of these sets of variables.

of participation, especially under the principal rubric *association*. In the next section, I examine the factors of wanting to make a difference as well as tax incentives.

---

## Identification: Love of neighbor and love of self

The social-psychological dispositions referred to in Exhibit 7.1 as "frameworks of consciousness" range from religious and political aspirations on the one hand to guilt and desire for control on the other. But the most formative, durable, and effective framework of consciousness—and the eventual outcome of guilt, duty, and other motives—is captured by the notion of identification. For wholesaler Dwyer, identifying with a cause is the criterion he uses to determine the causes to which his major contributions go. For instance, the fact that he "can fully identify" with the one-on-one drug rehabilitation program started by a local judge leads him to support the program with a series of major gifts. "I feel like I'm involved and a participant and I feel I can identify with the project, and I've learned enough about it to have some feeling that it's worth doing."

The key to care and philanthropy, as I have written elsewhere (for example, Schervish, 1993), is not the absence of self that motivates charitable giving but the presence of self-identification with others. This is what Thomas Aquinas teaches as the convergence of love of neighbor, love of self, and love of God. In its civic expression, it is what Tocqueville meant by "self-interest properly understood," and what Washington, D.C., respondent Dean Ehrlich expresses in personalistic terms as his and his wife's attraction to those causes "we can be identified with in order to give part of ourselves to." Recognizing the unity of self-development and community development has become the touchstone for Malcolm Hirsch's modest assessment of his giving, which he characterizes as "no big deal" and "not particularly generous." Rather, says the Tacoma environmental activist, "giving was just a front for figuring out who I was."

In this way, the inspiration for charitable giving and care in general is a function of the social-psychological processes of personal identification. It is for this reason that I have found that donors contribute the bulk of their charitable dollars to causes from whose services the donors directly benefit. It is not by coincidence that schools, health and arts organizations, and (especially) churches attract so much giving. For it is here that donors, because they are also recipients, most identify with the individuals—namely themselves, their families, and people much like them—whose needs are being met by the contributions. Although describing this form of giving as *consumption philanthropy* (Schervish, in press) may seem to discount its value, my intention is just the opposite. Within the identification model, consumption philanthropy is an honorable prototype of motivation to be emulated rather than a regrettable stereotype to be eschewed. Consumption philanthropy mobilizes charitable giving so formidably because it is here that identification between donor and recipient is strongest.

For generating generosity, the question is how to expand those same sentiments of identification to human beings in wider fields of space and time, that is, to extend the sentiments of family-feeling to the realms of fellow-feeling. This is the key to *adoption philanthropy* (see Schervish, 1992), where donors support individuals on the basis of a feeling of surrogate kinship. Again, it is not by coincidence that the golden rule entreats us to love our neighbor as ourselves.

"I listen and I go where I'm needed," says New York philanthropist Laura Madison. "The only thing I'm interested in in the world is the health of humanity. To be human is to be a spiritual person as well as a physical, mental, emotional person. This means to really relate to other human beings all over the world—whoever they are, wherever they are," she explains, highlighting how she extends her identification beyond her immediate sphere. Her goal is "making a oneness in every way that's there but isn't seen by most people—healing the earth, healing the rifts between people, all that sort of thing: that's what I'm really interested in. And wherever I see any chance or see that I'm supposed to be doing something about it, that's what I'm interested in." For Madison, the sentiments of identification derive from her perception of being needed; for Chicagoan Nancy Shaw they derive from her humanistic rendition of the golden rule, which she "professes" as her only religion. "I feel that you have a certain debt to society, and if you are comfortable, you pay it. And this is my way of doing it. I treat people as I would like to be treated. And that's as close to a religion as I can get." The religious undertones and concrete expressions of identification are what New York industrialist Stryker recalls his father teaching him as the way human beings live on after their deaths. "My father used to say—and this is not original with him—that he believed that each human being has a hereafter, and that it is not amorphous, not in heaven. It is tangible, palpable, measurable. And it consists of all the people who you've touched in your life for better or worse and who live on after."

---

## Association: The school of identification

The disposition of identification does not grow in isolation. The school of identification is the constellation of communities and organizations in which donors learn about the needs of the people with whom they (the donors) come to identify. Among our most consistent findings from over a decade of research is that the greatest portion of giving and volunteering takes place in one's own community and church and helps support activities from which the donor is directly associated. This means that the basis for higher giving and volunteering is in large part a function of the mix and intensity of the network of formal and informal associations both within and beyond one's local community. Over the course of our research, it has become increasingly clear that differences in levels of giving of time and money are due to more than differences in income, wealth, religion, gender, and race. When it comes to philanthropy, it is less a matter of financial capital, or even moral capital in the form of some kind of intrinsic faculty of generosity. What matters more is one's abundance of *associational capital* in the form of social networks, invitation, and identification.

For instance, 53-year-old hotel supplier Benjamin Ellman became ever more serious about volunteering his time and money to the Association of Jewish Community Centers as he came to associate with the clients of the centers. "It was unbelievable what I learned about the numbers of people in this community literally whose life depended on that agency," says Ellman. "I mean [they would have suffered gravely] if they didn't get the subvention so their kids could go to camps, or their kids could be in day care centers, or some of their older people could be taken care of in the elderly homes and got meals. I mean, their whole life depended on this institution." Indeed, it meant so much to him that he was able to see "where children have gone on from very humble beginnings to becoming major contributors not only to themselves but back to the community," that he eventually served two terms as president of the association.

New York philanthropist Janet Arnold traces her empathy for the least advantaged to her childhood when she and her siblings "were exposed to a wide variety of people and taught by both our parents the dignity of the human being. I think that was the foundation of my attitudes," she explains. The people who worked for her parents were always treated well. When she was young, her father took her along on his Latin American travels, where he would "go into the villages and talk to the people": "He loved going into the villages. He was wonderful with these people. He used to take us on trips, he worked in Latin America, and because of that, we were exposed to people who were not wealthy. We didn't move in a very narrow circle the way most people of wealth do, but a much wider circle through travel and because of my father's constantly reaching out to the people. And all of us, my brothers and sisters and I, worked in Latin America in summer jobs."

Arnold also spent years living among the poor and disguising her wealth on the east side of Detroit: "I loved being there and I loved working with those people. I guess I discovered that I had a very abiding belief in the potential of human beings, and that was something I wanted to affirm in my philanthropic work," she recalls. To this day, Arnold grounds her substantial philanthropic efforts on these formative experiences and has come to direct all her endeavors to "enabling people to grow and to achieve their potential." Again, it is her associational relations that put her face-to-face with those in need and that are the occasion for developing the necessary knowledge and desire for her major efforts to initiate small beginnings. "There are people who do small entrepreneurial things in their neighborhoods and they could use help," she explains. "To make their lives somehow successful [on their] own terms seems to me to be very important. You know, having better schools for children so that the children who grow up in Detroit or in Harlem, so their lives won't be circumscribed because they can't read."

Association also turns out to be the training ground of identification for Boston condominium builder Walter Adams, who purposefully guides his charitable giving by the maxim that "charity begins at home." He is grateful to his alma mater for making him conscientious, and to his employees for making him prosperous. So he directs his wealth to improving their fortunes. His major conventional charity is Boston College. But even closer to home and more worthy of Adams's attention are his workers, especially those at the lower end of the pay scale. He tells how instead of giving $100,000 to the United Way, he prefers to allocate that sum in order "to help some of [my] people who are in the lower end. Give them a bonus, I mean, or take $100,000 and hire a couple of truly nonemployables."

Ultimately there is nothing mysterious or extraordinary about the centrality of association in determining the amount and kinds of charitable engagements. "All giving is local" is an accurate portrayal of how charitable activity gets mobilized in and around the formal and informal social relations with which one is incorporated. Such incorporation may be direct, as occurs in and around one's church and university, or one's children's school or sports team. Incorporation may also be more indirect, for instance when the medical or mental illness suffered by a family member induces support for medical research to cure that illness. Association is even more indirect, but equally powerful, when the inspiration for contributions of time and money arrives through the media, as often occurs when news of famines and natural disasters attracts our care. Indeed, our own research (Schervish and Havens, 1997) and that of others (for example, Jackson, Bachmeier, Wood, and Craft, 1995) indicate that among all the variables listed in Exhibit 7.1, the strongest immediate determinant of charitable giving is the level of formal and informal engagement.

## Major purposes, major wealth, major taxes

I have described the individuality and principality that constitute the hyperagency of determination and dominion by which wealth holders shape the world. I have also explored the forces of identification and association that motivate their philanthropic engagement. In this section, I spell out how hyperagency and philanthropic motivation interact as wealth holders become major donors. First, I address the great expectations by which major donors seek to make a major difference. Second, I look at how growth in wealth and the estate tax code unite to mold a relatively powerful incentive for wealth holders to allocate large sums to philanthropy.

### Major purposes: Great expectations to make a major difference

The definition of wealth holders as hyperagents with personal determination and institutional dominion directly applies to their activity in the realm of philanthropy. Self-construction and world building do not stop at the doors to their homes or their businesses. It extends to all their involvements, including (for those who so choose) politics, community, religion, and philanthropy. By dint of personality, the wealthy are no more egoistically myopic or socially responsible than anyone else. Great expectations and grand aspirations occupy people across the financial spectrum. What is different for wealth holders is that they can legitimately be more confident about actualizing their expectations and aspirations because they are able to directly effect the fulfillment of their desires. It's a matter of realizing "how much a little money can make a difference," as Californian Francis Toppler puts it.

Hyperagency in philanthropy does not mean that the wealthy always and everywhere conceive or achieve major innovative interventions. It means they tend to think more about doing so, and to partake more in bringing them about. Entrepreneurs, said Brendan Dwyer, are investors who have two characteristics. First, they have a creative idea. They discern an area of output for which demand outstrips supply. Second, entrepreneurs are investors who actively affect the rate of return on their investment by directly commanding production. Correspondingly, venture capitalists are investors who bolster the capacity for others to be entrepreneurs. In business, wealth is an output. In philanthropy, wealth is an input. As such, wealth holders are the entrepreneurs and venture capitalists of philanthropic endeavors.

The distinctive class trait of the wealthy in philanthropy is the ability to bring into being, and not just support, particular charitable projects. Hyperagency in the field of philanthropy assigns financial resources to fabricating major outcomes. When exercising this capacity, wealth holders are *producers* rather than supporters of philanthropy, underwriters rather than just contributors. Finding neglected social niches where needs are great and resources scarce is precisely Janet Arnold's craft: "I am involved in human rights and I tend to be more involved with the American Indian, at this particular time, than I am with other minorities," says the third-generation guardian of a Detroit fortune. She contributes to many other causes, but her "main focus is on the American Indian"and other "unpopular" issues. "I gravitate to areas that have need and have no access to support," she says, because it is especially there "I feel like I can make a difference."

In common parlance, we regularly speak of large and small contributors. Distinguishing between producers and supporters of philanthropy is a more functional distinction. Each philanthropic enterprise pursues resources in order to produce outcomes in response to social needs and interests. Most individuals respond to appeals for contributions in a manner parallel to how a consumer responds to the products or services of a business. That is, they are consumers or supporters rather than creators or architects of the enterprise whose goods and services they wish to receive. Only as a group acting formally or informally in concert can consumers and contributors determine the fate of a charitable endeavor. Because it is the accumulated support of many individuals, rather than of any particular single individual, that determines the existence and direction of a venture, each separate individual is at most a joint or collateral producer.

It is a different story altogether, however, when a wealthy contributor provides a sizable enough gift to actually shape the agenda of a charity or nonprofit institution. In this instance, the contributor may be termed a direct producer or architect. Such direct production, of course, cuts two ways, and so it is always important to discern the conditions under which philanthropic hyperagency produces care rather than control (see Schervish, forthcoming).

Laura Madison clearly appreciates the productive potential of her charitable giving. "Because I have a large amount of money to put in," she explains, "I have an opportunity to really make a difference if I see something that a large amount of money could do more for than a small amount of money could." The extreme case of direct production is the personal founding of an original philanthropic organization or project. Such hyperagency gets exercised formally through creation of a private or working foundation, or through contribution of enough resources to establish within an existing organization a novel direction, such as a clinic, endowed chair, or hospital wing. Less formally, individuals of means can directly produce philanthropic outcomes by "adopting" specific individuals (including family members), organizations, or causes that they assist in a sufficiently large manner as to "make a difference."

It is precisely the possibility and practice of "making a difference" that undergirds the determination and dominion of hyperagency that marks Brendan Dwyer's charitable giving. "Whatever success I've got, and whatever I've learned, and whatever I get my satisfaction from come from being able to make a difference," says Dwyer. "That's what makes me happy: when I've felt I've made a difference in a beneficial way." Establishing a personal foundation as one vehicle for his charitable giving is only a small part of his institution-shaping philanthropy. He also contributes substantially enough to be considered a producer of the work of two university-based research institutes, a metro Detroit prison rehabilitation program, an inner-city charter school, and an inner-city church-based community organization. In the end, Dwyer counsels, there are two fairly straightforward questions that, if answered in the affirmative, mark the path of inclination that leads to philanthropy: "Is there something valuable you want to do that needs to be done in society? And can you do it better than Uncle Sam?"

### Major wealth: The expanding horizon of riches

Coupled to this inclination to make a difference in a major way is the opportunity to do so. Major donors have the inclination to fashion society; they also have the material wherewithal and tax incentive to do so.

The notion that philanthropy is indispensable for innovation in providing material goods and services for people in need, and for promoting cultural, social, and human capital for all members of society, is neither new nor controversial. What is new is the remarkable burgeoning in the material and (as I discuss in the conclusion) spiritual resources that may be devoted to philanthropy.

At the material level, there is clear evidence of growth in wealth. Despite a bifurcation between the lower and upper ends of the income and wealth distributions, growth in national wealth is outpacing growth in population by a factor of two, with per capita wealth growing around 5 percent per year. There are now close to four million millionaires and dramatically new conditions of affluence among the top 30 percent of the income and wealth distributions. There is much important rethinking and policy work to be done regarding issues of equity. For instance, contrary to conventional opinion, there is some indication that, when social security and private pensions are included, wealth has not become dramatically more concentrated in the seven decades since the depression (Wolff, 1996). But even among those who remain concerned about the level of concentration of wealth, no one seriously expects that major changes in the distribution of wealth are in the offing, even if we were to institute the most progressive *realistic* tax and transfer reforms.

On the contrary, there is every indication that the percentage of affluent and wealthy households will continue to grow, as every 1,000-point jump in the Dow Jones Industrial Average represents an increment of $1 trillion of wealth. The upshot is that there are larger and larger numbers of American households with the resources for modest-to-substantial philanthropic giving. It is the first time in history that large proportions of a population can materially afford to consider charitable giving as a principal component of their financial strategy and moral agency. A parallel trend is revealed in the 1993 study of Federal Reserve wealth data by researchers at Cornell University (Avery and Rendall, 1993). Avery and Rendall estimate that baby boomers ranging in age from thirty to forty-nine will share a $10 trillion transfer from their aging parents. Not surprisingly, much attention in philanthropic circles has been devoted to this transfer, which is projected to occur over the next three decades. (The dollar figure for this intergenerational transfer varies depending in part on how far into the future one is forecasting and on the rate of growth in wealth one assumes.)

Hoping to secure their share of this windfall, fundraisers and nonprofit professionals understandably have riveted their attention on three ideas. First, a disproportionate share (25–35 percent) of the intergenerational transfer will occur among the wealthiest

1.5–2 percent of the population (those with assets over $600,000). Second, this intergenerational transfer has the potential to unleash vast sums of money for philanthropic purposes. Third, because those who possess an inordinately high percentage of wealth have a considerably broader range of choices, it is therefore imperative to remind the patrons of this windfall about their choices and acquaint them with their charitable responsibilities. A fourth point, one made by financial planner Stephen Nill, is that "the bell curve of wealth release is already rapidly expanding, climbing from $39.4 billion in 1990 to $84.3 billion in 1995. The release will peak in 2015" (personal communication with author). Finally, a significant finding from our most recent research is that between 32 and 42 percent (depending upon the method of calculation) of all charitable contributions are currently given by the wealthiest 3.5 percent of the population (Schervish and Havens, in press). But even among the super-wealthy and upper affluent who make up this 3.5 percent of the population, there is surprising variation in the amounts given—suggesting a potential for increased giving among many at the upper reaches of income and wealth (see also Auten and Rudney, 1990).

### Major taxes: Incentives for major gifts

Perhaps the strongest material incentive for channeling this burgeoning major wealth to major gifts revolves around making positive use of the current estate tax laws. Much research has explored the effect of marginal income tax rates and other factors on the level of charitable giving from *income*, most recently a report prepared by Price Waterhouse for the Council on Foundations and INDEPENDENT SECTOR (1997) that confirms the positive effect of the charitable deduction on the amount of income given by individuals. However, we are only now beginning to recognize the implications of the growth in wealth for charitable giving from *wealth*. As I said, one of the emerging determinants of substantial giving from *wealth* among upper-income earners and wealth holders is the estate tax environment instituted by the 1986 changes in the federal tax code. Something that is now patently obvious to financial planners, tax accountants, and increasing numbers of wealthy individuals (especially small-business holders) is that the 1986 tax code dramatically increased the incentives of wealthy individuals to make substantial contributions to charity in lieu of paying an effective minimum wealth tax of at least 60 percent (see Murphy and Schervish, 1995). It is crucial to learn how current estate tax laws influence wealth holders to choose to dedicate their wealth (both while alive and at their death) to charity rather than government. As experienced financial planners such as Richard Haas, Scott Fithian, and Stuart Miller all insist, the only significant tax shelter for the very wealthy is philanthropy. Therefore, informing the affluent and wealthy about the practical tax advantages of the estate tax codes and about corresponding financial planning strategies that highlight charitable giving is one increasingly crucial and productive task.

## Conclusion: Spirituality in the age of affluence

Many wealthy and affluent individuals (especially among professionals and first-generation entrepreneurs) have not been adequately called upon to chart their resources for philanthropy. For the most part, the philanthropic community has not initiated effective strategies to persuade the financially well-off to make philanthropy the positive cornerstone for innovative and efficient production of valuable social outcomes. There are many reasons for this. In addition to not realizing their level of discretionary wealth (see for example Rosenberg, 1994, and Havens, 1996a, 1996b) and the positive implications of the current estate tax code, another serious obstacle is that potential major donors simply do not appreciate fully enough how effective charitable organizations are in generating valuable outcomes. As I said, one direction is to encourage fundraisers to become educated and then to educate their donors about the new social conditions of wealth and estate planning. But equally important is making donors cognizant of the effectiveness of their contributions. We believe this can best be achieved by incorporating donors into the associational relations that occur in and around charitable organizations. This is clearly congruent with our findings on participation and identification, which show the strategic importance of (1) involving donors in increasingly more engaging and rewarding participatory activities, (2) closely listening to what donors say about their areas of interest and welcoming them to contribute to such areas, and (3) bringing donors into relations of identification with the ultimate beneficiaries of their gifts.

This chapter has reviewed the material dominion and psychological determination of wealth holders. It has also discussed how growth in wealth in conjunction with the estate tax codes and the inclination of the wealthy to make a difference are positive vectors in the "physics of philanthropy." But as powerful as the forces are, it is the expansion of the spiritual potential for philanthropy that may prove to be the most significant factor. In a provocative 1930 essay entitled "Economic Possibilities for Our Grandchildren," John Maynard Keynes predicted that material wealth has the potential for releasing spiritual wealth. "The *economic problem* [of scarcity] may be solved, or at least within sight of solution, within a hundred years," Keynes wrote. "When the accumulation of wealth is no longer of high social importance, there will be great changes in the code of morals . . . such that the love of money as a possession—as distinguished from the love of money as a means to the enjoyments and realities of life—will be recognized for what it is, a somewhat disgusting morbidity, one of those semi-criminal, semi-pathological propensities which one hands over with a shudder to the specialists in mental disease" (1933, pp. 369–370).

For those concerned with understanding the spiritual potential in the new "code of morals" and mobilizing it in the service of philanthropy, much needs to be learned about harnessing what I call *spirituality in the age of affluence.* One strategy is to help fashion a philanthropic vocation for Keynes's grandchildren, who are now coming of financial age. To the extent that the affluent and wealth holders desire to search out their philanthropic vocation, there is a verdant opportunity to assist them in determining the socially beneficial charitable projects through which they may forge their moral identity. Given the tax environment, it is not unreasonable to expect that when they stop to reflect, the affluent and wealth holders will increasingly entertain the two questions formulated by Brendan Dwyer: Do you have something you want to accomplish for society? And do you think that philanthropic institutions can do a better job than government in accomplishing it?

The practical matter before us, then, is how to increase the probability that the answers to these questions are in the affirmative and in the service of society. This means working to produce and distribute a denser *social* capital of associational ties and a deeper *spiritual* capital of care. It also means doing so not just in the conventionally designated realms of giving and volunteering but in all the nooks—great and small—of our homes, communities, and world.

## References

Auten, G., and Rudney, G. "The Variability of Individual Charitable Giving in the U.S." *Voluntas: International Journal of Voluntary and Nonprofit Organizations*, 1990, *1* (2), 80–97.

Avery, R. B., and Rendall, M. S. "Estimating the Size and Distribution of Baby Boomers' Prospective Inheritances." Ithaca, N.Y.: Department of Economics, Cornell University, 1993.

Council on Foundations and INDEPENDENT SECTOR. *Impact of Tax Restructuring on Tax-Exempt Organizations.* Report prepared by the Washington National Tax Service of Price Waterhouse and by Caplin and Drysdale Chartered. Washington, D.C.: INDEPENDENT SECTOR, 1997.

Havens, J. J. "The Composition of Wealth and Charitable Giving." Working chapter. Boston College Social Welfare Research Institute, 1996a.

Havens, J. J. "Consumer Finances as Basis for Estimating Discretionary Income." Report submitted for the Indiana University Center on Philanthropy Discretionary Income Study, 1996b.

Hodgkinson, V. A., and Weitzman, M. A. Giving and Volunteering in the United States: Findings from a National Survey. Washington, D.C.: INDEPENDENT SECTOR, 1992.

Jackson, E. F., Bachmeier, M. D., Wood, J. R., and Craft, E. A. "Volunteering and Charitable Giving: Do Religious and Associational Ties Promote Helping Behavior?" *Nonprofit and Voluntary Sector Quarterly*, 1995, *24* (1), 59–78.

Keynes, J. M. "Economic Possibilities for our Grandchildren." *Essays in Persuasion.* London: Macmillan, 1933.

Murphy, T. B., and Schervish, P. G. "The Dynamics of Wealth Transfer: Behavioral Implications of Tax Policy for the $10 Trillion Transfer." Presented at the INDEPENDENT SECTOR 1995 Spring Research Forum, "Nonprofit Organizations as Public Actors: Rising to New Public Policy Challenges," Alexandria, Va., Mar. 23–24, 1995.

Ostrander, S. A., and Schervish, P. G. "Giving and Getting: Philanthropy as a Social Relation." In J. Van Til (ed.), *Critical Issues in American Philanthropy: Strengthening Theory and Practice.* San Francisco: Jossey-Bass, 1990.

Rosenberg, C., Jr. *Wealthy and Wise: How You and America Can Get the Most out of Your Giving.* New York: Little, Brown, 1994.

Schama, S. *The Embarrassment of Riches: An Interpretation of Dutch Culture in the Golden Age.* Berkeley: University of California Press, 1988.

Schervish, P. G. "Adoption and Altruism: Those with Whom I Want to Share a Dream." *Nonprofit and Voluntary Sector Quarterly,* 1992, *21* (4), 327–350.

Schervish, P. G. "Philanthropy as a Moral Identity of *Caritas.*" In P. G. Schervish with O. Benz, P. Dulany, T. B. Murphy, and S. Salett, *Taking Giving Seriously.* Indianapolis: Indiana University, Center on Philanthropy, 1993.

Schervish, P. G. "The Moral Biographies of the Wealthy and the Cultural Scripture of Wealth." In P. G. Schervish (ed.), *Wealth in Western Thought: The Case for and Against Riches.* New York: Praeger, 1994.

Schervish, P. G. "Gentle as Doves and Wise as Serpents: The Philosophy of Care and the Sociology of Transmission." In P. G. Schervish, V. A. Hodgkinson, and M. Gates (eds.), *Care and Community in Modern Society: Passing on the Tradition of Care to the Next Generation.* San Francisco: Jossey-Bass, 1995.

Schervish, P. G. "Inclination, Obligation, and Association: What We Know and What We Need to Learn about Donor Motivation." In D. F. Burlingame (ed.), *Critical Issues in Fund Raising.* New York: Wiley, 1997.

Schervish, P. G. *The Modern Medicis: Strategies of Philanthropy Among the Wealthy.* San Francisco: Jossey-Bass, in press.

Schervish, P. G., and Havens, J. J. "Social Participation and Charitable Giving: A Multivariate Analysis." *Voluntas: International Journal of Voluntary and Nonprofit Organizations,* 1997, *8*(3).

Schervish, P. G., and Havens, J. J. "Money and Magnanimity: New Findings on the Distribution of Income, Wealth, and Philanthropy." *Nonprofit Management & Leadership,* in press.

Schervish, P. G., and Herman, A. *Empowerment and Beneficence: Strategies of Living and Giving Among the Wealthy.* Final report, the Study on Wealth and Philanthropy. Presentation of findings from the Study on Wealth and Philanthropy, submitted to the T. B. Murphy Foundation Charitable Trust, 1988.

Wolff, E. N. "International Comparisons of Wealth Inequality." *Review of Income and Wealth,* 1996, *42* (4), 433–451.

PAUL G. SCHERVISH *is director of the Social Welfare Research Institute and professor of sociology at Boston College.*

# Index

# Ordering Information

NEW DIRECTIONS FOR PHILANTHROPIC FUNDRAISING is published quarterly in Fall, Winter, Spring, and Summer and is available for purchase by subscription and individually.

SUBSCRIPTIONS cost $67.00 for individuals (a savings of 33 percent over single-copy prices) and $115.00 for institutions, agencies, and libraries. Prices subject to change. Please do not send institutional checks for personal subscriptions. Standing orders are accepted. (For subscriptions outside of North America, add $7.00 for shipping via surface mail or $25.00 for air mail. Orders *must be prepaid* in U.S. dollars by check drawn on a U.S. bank or charged to VISA, MasterCard, or American Express.)

SINGLE COPIES cost $25.00 plus shipping (see below) when payment accompanies order. California, New Jersey, New York, and Washington, D.C., residents please include appropriate sales tax. Canadian residents add GST and any local taxes. Billed orders will be charged shipping and handling. No billed shipments to post office boxes. (Orders from outside North America *must be prepaid* in U.S. dollars by check drawn on a U.S. bank or charged to VISA, MasterCard, or American Express.)

SHIPPING (SINGLE COPIES ONLY): $30.00 and under, add $5.50; to $50.00, add $6.50; to $75.00, add $7.50; to $100.00, add $9.00; to $150.00, add $10.00.

DISCOUNTS for quantity orders are available. Please write to the address below for information.

ALL ORDERS must include either the name of an individual or an official purchase order number. Please submit your order as follows:
>    *Subscriptions:* specify series and year subscription is to begin
>    *Single copies:* include individual title code (such as PF1)

MAIL ORDERS TO: Jossey-Bass Publishers, 350 Sansome Street, San Francisco, California 94104–1342.

PHONE subscription or single-copy orders toll-free at (888) 378-2537 or at (415) 433-1767 (toll call).

FAX orders toll-free to (800) 605-2665.

# Previous Issues Available